FAITH ON THE WAY

FAITH ON THE WAY

A practical parish guide to the
Adult Catechumenate

PETER BALL
and
MALCOLM GRUNDY

MOWBRAY
London and New York

Mowbray
A Continuum imprint

The Tower Building   370 Lexington Avenue
11 York Road   New York
London SE1 7NX   NY 10017–6503

First published 2000

British Library Cataloguing-in-Publication Data
A catalogue record for this book is available from the British Library.

ISBN   0–264–67528–2

Designed and typeset by Kenneth Burnley, Wirral, Cheshire
Printed and bound in Great Britain by TJ International, Padstow, Cornwall

CONTENTS

FOREWORD

I AM DELIGHTED TO COMMEND THIS BOOK as a valuable resource for clergy and lay people who accompany enquirers and new Christians on the early stages of the journey in faith.

As a parish priest in urban Portsmouth and as Chairman of the Liturgical Commission at a time when our church's rites of initiation have been substantially revised, I know personally the value of this catechumenal approach in preparing adult enquirers for the sacraments of baptism and confirmation and for others exploring again a renewed commitment to faith.

Also, from my participation in the working party which produced *On the Way* and from our work in the Liturgical Commission on rites to accompany those who are on the way, I am aware of the coherence and power of the approach presented by Peter Ball and Malcolm Grundy, expressing what it means to be Church, focused on the common life of all the baptized.

They bring to *Faith on the Way* the many years of the Catechumenate Network's experience and expertise. Anglican awareness of the catechumenate looks back to beginnings in the early 1970s and draws on insights from widely different parochial and pastoral contexts. Links with fellow workers across Western Europe, from Sweden to Italy, from Ireland to the Czech Republic, in the United States, Australia and New Zealand, all bring their own richness.

The roots of *Faith on the Way*, essentially in the primary sacrament of baptism, are to be found in the practice of the undivided Church. Part of the mission of this movement is to renew awareness of baptism in and for the whole Church. It is our one baptism in Christ that unites us all, even though the churches may remain divided in other ways.

Faith on the Way is designed to be a useful and practical handbook for parish teams, with material that can be photocopied for use in training. It follows the success of the authors' earlier work in this field, and offers the first drafts of work from the Liturgical Commission for use in celebrating the stages of the journey and key moments in people's development of faith, commitment and understanding. These services have their origins in the report *On the Way: Towards an Integrated Approach to Christian Initiation* (Church House Publishing, 1995), which was drafted by a group drawn from the Board of Mission, the Board of Education and the Liturgical Commission. That membership indicates the breadth of support for this kind of approach to being Church in the twenty-first century, and I warmly commend the authors' work.

THE RT REVD DR DAVID STANCLIFFE
Bishop of Salisbury

PREFACE

THIS BOOK ARISES from our own experience of accompanying others on their journey to a deeper faith. It is also a part of our own faith story. We have come to discover more of how the pressures and joys of life feed our own spirituality. It is in exploring, and wrestling with, life's questions that we come to discover the strength of God's presence in our lives. We have also had to share our journey in a church, with its many denominations, which has had to undergo many changes and ask deep questions about its own ways of working. Our life in the Adult Catechumenate movement has been both at the heart of the church and at its edge. We hope that some of our searching and our offering will be experienced as this book is read.

The chapters of this book are designed for use in local church communities. They have been written for ordained and lay Christians who accompany adults on their journey into a deeper faith.

Faith on the Way has grown out of our own commitment and experience, but is also deeply indebted to countless parishioners, friends and colleagues for their encouragement and support. Some sections draw upon work previously published in Peter Ball's *Adult Way to Faith* (Mowbray, 1992) and Malcolm Grundy's *Understanding Congregations* (Mowbray, 1998). Those pieces of writing have been our way of marking stages on our way. This present book has been written from where we think we might be now on our journey.

The worksheets which are found at the end of several of the chapters are meant to be used. So we are more than happy for them to be photocopied for local use in the training and development of people in the methods we describe. Please acknowledge this book as their source.

PETER BALL
MALCOLM GRUNDY

ONE

HOW SHALL WE EVER LEARN?

D O WE EVER LEARN from our mistakes? What do we learn when so often we seem to repeat the same mistakes again? What is the difference between information and knowledge? If we know all the facts, will we necessarily make the wisest of decisions? Questions like these are at the heart of discovering how adults learn. Answers are part of what we have learned from our experience of working with 'Faith on the Way'.

In this book we set out our ideas for bringing adults to faith. In doing this we want to tell, through our own story, how our use of the Adult Catechumenate draws on good learning practice and the insights of spiritual direction. We call this method of working with people 'Faith on the Way'.

There is now such a bank of information available to us that any fact commonly available can be brought up on a computer screen within seconds. Yet information gathering, the amassing of facts, is not learning. There is a great truth in the realization that the more we come to know in our heads and hearts, the more we become aware of how little we know. There is a wise saying which points to a paradoxical truth that education is what is left when we have forgotten all that we ever learned.

In the same way, living and praying the Christian life is more than knowing about the Bible, church history and the teachings and doctrines of the Church. It is more than understanding the finer points of the liturgy in its free-flow or its ritualistic choreography. It is more than knowing why vicars wear what they do in church and why there are different liturgical colours for different seasons, interesting and important as all these things are.

Journey

Many of the great world religions have the concept of pilgrimage at their heart. To visit Mecca or to travel to bathe in the Ganges are as significant in other faiths as a Holy Land pilgrimage is to many Christians. In much of our spirituality this theme has become very rich as new understandings of how we deepen our faith have been shared. For many people, the way to a deeper faith has been likened to a pilgrimage or journey. Geoffrey Chaucer found this a good medium for the tales of his Canterbury pilgrims, and John Bunyan used this allegory to describe our journey through life in his *Pilgrim's Progress*. In 'Faith on the Way' we interweave the two ideas of how adults learn and of life as a spiritual journey in the methods we use. This means that coming to faith is a slow progress. It is a pilgrimage which is made in the company of others. Stories are told and questions asked as we journey along the way. We discover together that both learning and the deepening of our faith are lifelong processes. At different stages of our lives we learn, react, accept or rebel according to who we are. We continue to ask questions about what has made us who we are, where we are now and what we might be able to anticipate as the consequences of our actions.

Do churchgoers want to learn?

Very few people look to their local church to be educated. Here, perhaps, is the difficulty which needs to be faced at the beginning of a book like ours. Those who have come close to a local congregation have come for a wide variety of very personal reasons. Some have come by accident or through loyalty to a friend, or under compulsion, but when they get there something is experienced which contradicts their illusions about the Church.

Jayne Ozanne has been conducting some challenging studies of attitudes towards the Church from outsiders. This work was commissioned and published by the Church of England Archbishops' Council under the title *Hopes and Dreams for a Future Church* (Ozanne, 2000). Young people said to her things like: 'The Church is scary, we don't understand it at all!', 'We don't trust the Church – it stresses me out!'.

When asked for animal associations, they said: 'Fluffy yellow chick: reminds of Easter'; 'Shire horse: nice to keep but out of date'; 'Dog: reminds me of the Queen and her corgi'; 'Magpie: always trying to get your money'; 'Dinosaur: used to cover a lot of areas'; 'Lion: lies in wait, pounces, rips you apart.'

An under-25-year-old churchgoer said 'We look silly, all doing the same thing together.' An under-25-year-old non-churchgoer said: 'Nice people but trapped.' From this and many other responses, Jayne Ozanne concluded:

> Their experience of Church stems primarily from school, where religion was 'forced on them'. They do not understand the purpose of 'chanting' and 'men with dresses', and view this with some fear. They are suspicious of the Church and its motives. They do not understand the freedom the gospel brings – they only see 'the rules and regulations'.

Our approach

We as authors, and many of our readers, will approach the Church, and respond to what other people say about it, from a particular point of view. This book comes from two authors who are convinced that adults learn, and learn about the Christian faith and the Church, in particular ways. We have written and revised parts of this book for those who may well be searching for a similar approach but who have not found a framework for their ideas and experiences. Indeed, hardly anyone is likely to buy or be given the book if they are not interested in helping adult enquirers deepen their faith through a reflective process of adult learning. We want to share our ideas and experiences about how to engage with others in this process.

Other approaches

If we may exaggerate a little, there are those who see the need to introduce people to the faith by telling them things, by explaining about the Bible and how it was put together, by telling them about Jesus and encouraging them to participate in the liturgy. They may want to encourage newcomers to join a confirmation group, house group or Lent course. The focus is often on imparting information to newcomers on subjects which we, who are already within the churches, think they will want to understand.

What do enquirers want?

Looked at from another point of view – that of the newcomer or passive church member – they are looking for something else. They want, as they might well say, to come into a church and soak up the silence, to 'recharge their batteries'. They may well be very apprehensive, full of the images and misrepresentations which Jayne Ozanne has revealed, but energized enough to want to begin to attend – and then to keep on coming. Church may be about childhood memories rekindled or it might be about the memory of a loved one recently lost. Coming to church might well be a combination of a series of chance coincidences (to them) where they have been encouraged by a friend or because the time is more appropriate in their lives to be able to come to church. Astonishingly, some people just appear off the street, like what they experience and want to come again. Some people make a few more friends than they would otherwise have.

When we reflect on the rainbow of reasons people will give for seeking a deeper faith, we conclude that there are some inner concepts they are searching for and are trying to discover and put into their lives.

Community, meaning and identity

They are looking for some *new experience* which will give more meaning and sense of purpose to their lives than they have at present. Many are willing to take on trust the apparent certainty about the meaning of life which a certain congregation possesses. Many people are looking for the sense that they can *belong to a community of people* who will offer them friendship and an often unspoken awareness that they share the same set of values. Modern life bombards us all with value systems which are often seen as confusing and in competition with one another. These differences are highlighted, for instance, over the issue of sexuality and the acceptance of a variety of personal relationships.

As a combination of the *search for meaning and community* many people have an underlying anxiety about their own sense of value or identity. We are recognized differently in the different aspects of our lives – at home, at work, by our parents or our children, by our friends and even in our churches. The truth is that we often behave like different people in the various places in which we find ourselves. On occasions we are forced to behave in certain ways which feel less than authentic to us and, acting out a role, we begin to ask, 'Who am I?'. Going into a church can bring us into a comforting situation where we feel we can be accepted and understood – we believe and want to be reassured that God knows who we really are.

If these understandings of why people come to church are in any way close to the mark, then enthusiastic, 'need to tell' recruiters and educators should beware. We need to be cautious, unless there is some understanding of what we have discovered and developed. Such a fundamental grasp will lead us to the sensitive understanding that we need to listen to newcomers and enquirers and to begin where they are. Trust and community building begins with the questions which newcomers are asking. Pre-prepared courses may be well packaged and look attractive, but they start from where we are and with the answers to the questions which we think that other people need.

The Adult Catechumenate, or 'Faith on the Way', starts with the assumption that conversion through the deepening of faith is a gradual process. It begins with the questions enquirers are asking. It provides a structured way in which believers and enquirers can make a journey of faith discovery together. It never teaches using a 'top down' approach and it never has pre-prepared answers. It understands that real learning only takes place when teacher and student, enquirer and sponsor, can exchange ideas and experiences with one another in an atmosphere of trust.

We have a lovely idea, as a parody of the ideal of education. Can we say that Christianity is what is left when we have forgotten all we ever learned about creeds, doctrine and ritual? We think we can, because that is what we see and understand of God when we look at the person and life of Jesus. His approach to the religious and political leaders of his day was to point those who came to him to the integral truth at the heart of their seeking, not to the correct observance of inherited ethical codes and the observance of a legalism which leads from one kind of slavery straight to another.

How can we take our own medicine?

For all of the thirty and more years of our lives as clergymen we have
been involved in the education of adults. Peter's training as a curate
on the large parish staff at All Saints, Poplar, in the East End of
London with a great deal of work with young people, was followed
by ministry as a parish priest in the suburbs of London where the
development of adult Christian education was a major interest,
together with a long-standing concern with the television industry as
chaplain to one of the major independent companies. More recently,
as a Cathedral Canon and in semi-retirement he has been engaged in
training and promotion with the Adult Catechumenate and in spiritual direction for a number of people.

For Malcolm the first eleven years were spent, as Senior Chaplain
of the Sheffield Industrial Mission, in discussion groups with
apprentices in the steel industry and at pit-head training centres near
to coal mines, now long closed. Then he moved on to sharing in and
subsequently organizing training for staff and managers. From that
time onwards his work has been to organize training events and offer
consultancy so that church members could learn more about their
faith and consider its implications. When he moved to work in
London in 1980 he discovered the Adult Catechumenate among
many other training facilities. From there he went on to begin Adult
Catechumenate groups as Team Rector of Huntingdon.

Those who lived through adult education in those days will
remember training methods which were called 'experiential'. We
went on conferences where the different parts of a day were called
'Session 1' or 'Session 2'. No one gave any input. The leaders were
called 'consultants' and offered the most meagre comments through
an evening, a day or a weekend. The dynamics of the group were
what was all important. We learned by interacting with one another
– often with no debriefing. To this present day, an element of that
experiential atmosphere survives.

The pendulum of fashion has swung considerably in many
training groups since those 'experience is all' days. Now there seems
to be an emphasis on 'input' and 'keynote speakers'. What were once
derided as 'string-of-pearls', speaker-after-speaker conferences are
now much more in fashion. In religion there seems to be a return to
the need to 'tell' people things.

Trends in any culture frequently determine the style of education. For very much more than a century, school and university education was delivered by a teacher or lecturer standing at the front with students sitting in rows of desks taking the wisdom down as if it were being delivered from God on High. This kind of lecturing has been described as the passing of information from the page of the lecturer to the page of the student without passing through the minds of either! The experiential method was tried with schoolchildren. Where once we all learned our multiplication tables by rote, our children learned to write and to calculate (or not) by what seemed more like play. It is all now shifting back again. The permissive sixties and seventies became the acquisitive eighties and the conformist nineties. What went for public educational methods went, and goes, also for religious education.

We shall end this chapter prefacing a description of 'Faith on the Way' by saying that we believe this is the very best method of bringing adults to a deeper faith. We shall get to that conclusion by looking at the way in which we have discovered, through our own experience, how adults learn. We begin by giving an example from Malcolm's small rural village about a project to embroider new kneelers to go in church to commemorate the Millennium.

Kneelers for the Millennium

In the spring of 1999 the parishioners in the village decided to embroider kneelers to place in the pews of the local church as a celebration of the Millennium. The kneelers can be purchased in kit form. They come with a design printed on canvas and enough of the right-coloured woollen threads to complete the picture. In the pack is a foam block and a hessian square for the backing. Once the pattern is completed the kneeler is made by sewing the sides and back. A label is enclosed so that the name of the embroiderer or the dedication can be written in. Designs for a kneeler can be selected from a catalogue or can be printed by the suppliers on request.

The whole project was a tremendous success. Over 130 kneelers were produced. Churchgoers began with some enthusiasm. When others in the village heard of what was happening they wanted to purchase kits or to have a kneeler embroidered for them, often in memory of a friend or relative. The assistant bishop of the diocese came for a special service to bless the completed work and to attend a lunch afterwards. The local press took photographs. A couple in the village devised a project on their computer whereby kneeler designs could be made. They put the village, the church and the kneelers, on the Internet for all to see. It became hard to stop even more villagers wanting kneelers.

A learning process

Soon after this project got under way Malcolm realized that there were many different pieces of learning happening all together. It could be useful to analyse them and reflect on the processes, and so to understand and apply the different types of learning for varied activities in the life of a local church. These learning activities are little different from learning which takes place in any other organization. The differences, so far as they can be discerned, are in the context of a small rural village, the culture of a local church and the relationship of religion to a task-focused piece of work.

He could see that there were at least twelve sub-divisions in the learning process:

1. *The topic idea.* This connects with a largely secular event, the Millennium celebration, and attempts to bring a religious theme into the marking of this by a village. The idea of sewing our own kneelers is suggested and organized by a member of the community who had organized a similar scheme in the place where she lived before. So, to some extent, there was prior learning and experience. It had to be adapted and re-worked to come fresh as their own idea to the people of this village.

2. *Product information.* A well-known national company produces catalogues of kits with instructions for making them up. Kits are available by mail order. The company advertises in the church press. No church members take such newspapers, so information has to be shared by the member of the congregation who knows how to find the advertisement.

3. *Promotion and collection of orders.* The main enthusiast for the scheme gets leaflets and shows them around. She makes up a sample kneeler to show others what the finished product is like. It is important to have a mental, and sometimes practical, picture of the outcome. It unites people around a common ideal. She

takes a list of those interested, and collects orders and money – a learning and organizing process in itself. At this stage there is liaison with the local clergy to gain assent for the project. The clergy then have to liaise with the church authorities to gain permission for such a significant change to the internal appearance of the church. In all of these activities new areas of exploration are undertaken, new levels of authority approached and confidence built up.

4. *Project organization.* Once the scale of the number of kneelers became known there emerged the need to keep a close record of orders and an account of the finance. Kneelers had to be ordered and paid for in advance. There was a cash-flow problem solved by my own credit card facility! Negotiation had to take place for the non-stitchers to get their kneelers made up. Not every villager was thought suitable to sew anyone's kneeler. Tradition, memory, resentment – and sometimes forgiveness – came into play. Distribution and collection had to be organized.

5. *Learning how to sew.* Some in the village took to the sewing like professionals and were turning out kneelers as on a production line. Others had to re-visit skills long unused. A few had to keep on asking and telephoning for reassurance. Was it acceptable for men to embroider? Some could embroider the pattern but had to ask others to sew the kits together. The inventive drew new pictures on plain backcloths and designed their own. In this way some village pictures and some local industries were recorded.

6. *Design and develop.* Once it was understood that there was permission to design, imagination blossomed. Some people drew their designs and sewed them up themselves while others found a friend to do the drawing. A younger couple who had recently moved into the village offered their computer skills to design a computer program and offered, for a price, this service to other churches. They achieved success in the considerable challenge of finding out how to advertise their service in the diocesan mailing! The same computer-literate people put the village, the church and the project on the Internet.

7. *Spill-over into school.* Pupils from the village school went to the church for a Millennium event and were shown the kneelers. They immediately wanted to have one from their school. The teachers were very willing to co-operate and it was agreed that a

volunteer who knew about making the kneelers would go in and supervise work in a lunchtime. Some children learned to sew for the first time. A volunteer discovered new supervision and teaching skills.

8. *Celebrating the achievement.* When an end to the main project could be foreseen, agreement had to be reached that the Bishop would be invited to bless the new kneelers. Considerable negotiation had to take place about whether he could be taken out to lunch by old friends of his who lived close by. There was a long wait to see if the local 'squire' would invite him to his house. Eventually it became clear that a lunch in the village hall was what would happen. In a community with considerable conservative tradition, a service had to be designed to suit most tastes.

9. *Organizing the lunch.* Another group had to bring their organizing skills into play to organize, and sell tickets for, a lunch.

10. *Getting publicity.* The two local newspapers (one in Lancashire and one in Yorkshire) had to be contacted and a photographer organized to take 'posed' pictures later in the week.

11. *Dealing with the fall-out.* Not everyone liked the project, not everyone agreed with the service, not everyone who booked came to the lunch . . . While some came more closely into church life, others took this as the opportunity to leave. Learning how to leave, and how to allow others to leave, is a skill in itself.

12. *Deciding how to end.* In a community project, with different people taking responsibility for different parts of the process, but with no designated overall leader, who decides and how do they decide that the project is to end? There comes a stage in a small country church when more than 130 kneelers seems superfluous – and, of course, not everyone agreed to throw out the old kneelers, so some had to be kept! Learning when to stop is a skill indeed.

That's how we learn

In that everyday story of a group of people developing a piece of community activity it is possible to make a list much longer than twelve of the different ways in which adults learn. We are not going to go on with that sub-division: it would be more tedious than the dullest lecture. What attracts and stimulates us to think more about adult learning is the way in which it is possible to 'cluster' together different experiences of learning. They can then be brought out for use according to the needs and composition of any group of people. That is what using the catechumenal process of adult learning is all about.

A number of our colleagues have reflected on this in their own writings. Yvonne Craig first developed the idea of 'villages of learning' in an article in the *British Journal of Theological Education* (1994). The ideas became more publicly known within the churches when *Tomorrow is Another Country* (General Synod Board of Education, 1996) was published. This book was described as 'very American' when extracts from it were used at an English theological college four years later!

Approaches to learning

As ever, the basic idea is very simple. The needs of people to get something done will determine the learning methods which are best to use. As with all pieces of educational material, the user has to take them in and make them their own. In what we outline below, we will try to show what we have done with this stimulating clustering of ideas in order to use them in training work.

Without our being aware of it, our instincts become developed in a way similar to that of our conscience. We have a certain kind of temperament. This is sometimes attributed to 'the way we are made'. We inherit certain traits from our parents. We react in quite a strong way to some of the patterns of behaviour used by our parents. Many of us were influenced by one schoolteacher or another and often use the techniques we admired in them. Yet others of us will have had a bad experience of school and of living up to its expectations. All of us who have grown into adulthood will testify to the many other ways we have learned through the life experiences we have had to cope with.

This mixture of temperament, our past history and our preferred way to survive in life all combine to form the 'cluster' of approaches we bring to any new task. Our adaptation of the 'villages of learning' idea has led us to create caricature names for the approaches people bring to learning. When this is appreciated it becomes clearer that congregations, like any other organization in society, need to develop different activities for a range of temperamentally varied members. When focusing on a task, like that of the kneeler project, different skills and abilities are offered by different members of a community in order to achieve an outcome which would have been impossible for a limited or exclusive group. Such caricatured or personalized approaches to learning can look like this:

- *The do-it-yourself home improver.* The learner is someone who needs to acquire skills in order to perform certain tasks. Whether it is home decoration or car maintenance, computer skills or sewing a kneeler, what is needed is 'know-how'. This is gained by looking at manuals and instruction books. It comes from attending adult education classes and from watching an 'expert' at work. We read on the packet about how to make bread, but we did not really see how to kneed the dough until we watched Delia Smith on the television!
- *The regular attender at evening classes or discussion groups.* The learner is committed and willing to continue to add information to his or her knowledge base. There are some people who just enjoy gleaning facts and exploring new subjects. Group members sometimes come because the 'leader' will tell them new things. Others come because they enjoy a good discussion – whatever the subject. Many people – more than we dare to admit – come for the company.
- *The person who likes lectures and reads factual books.* The learner is a container to be filled. There certainly are those who prefer to sit and listen and to make notes. The sitting-in-a-circle-and-sharing-experiences type of group is painfully alien to some people, for whatever reason. A lecture can convey facts, it can tell about an adventure or journey, it can inspire and create an atmosphere, it can inform and entertain. There are many who do not know the value of the learning and experience they already have and who feel that an 'expert' can tell them things which may then equip the hearer and give them confidence.
- *The radical campaigner.* This is the person who uses discussion groups to persuade others over to their point of view. Meetings need to have a purpose. Someone with a cause needs an audience to proclaim their views. They hope to convert the hearers by persuasive argument, often tinged with an emotional appeal. It is best to know the purpose of a meeting if it is of this kind. The radical campaigner with one agenda, not always stated, can be tedious in an 'open' discussion group. Alternatively, single–issue

groups, once formed, become effective through the focused activity of the group members.

- *The wine maker.* The learner here is a growing plant whose knowledge matures with development and refinement. We collect information and bring different sources together to make a richer whole. The in-depth study of a subject over many years can produce a person who is a mine of interesting information. This is at its best when uncorked and left to reach the same room temperature as the rest of the hearers.

- *The debater.* This is the person who will say there is always another point of view – and a personality type who will explore a contradictory position for its own sake. This is the wonderful atmosphere of the university common room. It can be stimulating and force us all to clarify and refine our ideas. It is tedious when it is an argument which only pretends to come from strongly held belief.

- *We need to be told.* This is the learner who feels inadequate and who prefers the secure framework set by someone else. Our good and bad experiences of formal education colour our approach to learning. It is easier, and sometimes more comforting, to just sit and listen. The passive listener can encourage the bore. A polite but searching question can make for a much more interesting evening. The person who cannot take a well-meant question or interruption should not be allowed to hold the floor. The really skilled enabler may begin with a talk but is able to move with consummate ease to drawing from others their comments and experiences. In that way we gain from others and grow in self-confidence.

- *The leader, the led and the organizer.* Here we have the person who learns through doing and often by organizing others into doing. There is a world of difference between the task addressed by 'Follow me' and the task achieved through corporate effort. Leadership which is sensitive and reflective moves from being 'up front' to uniting a group around a common task or objective. Equally, the person who learns through being organized into a workgroup may well be happy to be a servant or slave for a while. Leadership skills enable such people to grow in self-confidence and feel able to suggest even more interesting ways to carry out the simple task. It is always best for there to be clear lines of accountability and for a group to know how it is being organized. Even within the same group there can be different leaders for different tasks. When this works well, the true value of each member can be fully appreciated.

- *Can we find it in a book?* Latent within many teachers, group organizers and class or discussion group members is the desire to find the perfect course all within the covers of one book. Somewhere there will exist this 'made in heaven' text. It will require little or no preparation by the teacher, it will have easily accessible information at just the right level for all the class members, it will have easily understood diagrams and illustrations, and there will be helpful discussion-starters at the end of each chapter. At the end of each event all the members will go away with the feeling that they really have found something new in the session, that they have learned things, they have been listened to and that they will do new things with their lives as a result. Miracles do happen, teachers and learners become as one, society is transformed, pigs can fly.

    No one would admit to this in an open way, but deep down there seems to be some kind of resentment that learning, and the running of group sessions, needs preparation. Many people who attend events of the information-gathering kind imagine that they will take in and remember most of the information which is given to them.

How can all this fantasy-like series of approaches be harvested into real learning? The strength of the 'Faith on the Way' process is that it uses different kinds of learning according to the different kinds of questions the members of the local group are asking. There is no one book which will give all the answers. Even with the arrival of two particular 'courses', reflection on their use brings out the strength of the 'villages of learning' approach.

The packaged market leaders

The excitement of being within the life of many congregations at the moment is that many new people are coming to faith and into membership. As the confirmation of young people declines, the rise in the number of adults asking for membership increases. There is a genuine spiritual search and hunger among great numbers of people in many parts of the world. In Britain, and some parts of northern Europe, two significant training resources have come into use as adults are welcomed into local congregations. It is important for us to comment on them at this early stage in the advocacy of our own working methods.

Alpha courses

The popularity and wide use of Alpha courses hardly needs to be noted.[1] Churches of very different persuasions have taken to using Alpha both as a refresher for existing members and particularly as a welcoming method for enquirers. Reflection on the use of Alpha brings the most interesting paradox. Alpha is as close as it is possible to come to a packaged course with everything the local organizer will need. Indeed, it has the copyright protection of its authors and mar-keters. It is not difficult to use and has its own books and videos for the preparation and the running of each session. Authority is acknowledged. There is a brand name and style which is assimilated as users buy into the product.

Yet when Alpha group members are asked what they valued most about the sessions, they do not say the books, or the video or the Bible teaching – they say they found the shared meal the most important thing of all in the entire experience. They shared a meal and had open discussion with newly-made friends.

Alpha meets many needs and it is to be congratulated and encouraged. At a time when even the slightest knowledge of the Christian story cannot be assumed, Alpha scores highly on telling people who Jesus is. In an age where it is becoming increasingly difficult to make and maintain stable relationships, the Alpha meal and process enables new friendships to be made in an atmosphere of protective warmth which contrasts in many ways to members' experiences in a hostile, fragmented and consequently lonely world. Who would not look for easy solutions and an easy escape route from the oppressive nature of much of life?

The Emmaus course

If Alpha is a packaged introduction into the Christian faith, the Emmaus course offers a very well-resourced journey into a deeper faith (National Society with the Bible Society, 1998). It is highly

accomplished in putting into printed form the living experience of a
journey into faith. In Volume 1, if not later on in the material, there
is a clear starting point with a welcome which begins by listening to
the enquirer's experience and questions from life so far. Resource
books lead group members into the possibility of deep and personal
discussions about faith and the meaning of life. There is the opportunity for deeper commitment and the application of a new faith to the
workaday world. It is indeed a most helpful course and should be
considered by any congregation with life in it.

Sit down with a group of lay people and clergy who have used the
Emmaus course and they will say that there was just too much
printed material. Excellent resources handed out to group members
became abandoned as soon as discussion took off. Group members
wanted to begin with the questions they were asking, not with the
questions and answers which materials producers thought they
needed at this stage in their faith journey.

A real curate's egg – good in parts

Alpha and Emmaus are excellent. They have tapped into just where
enquirers are at the moment. In a world which yearns for certainty,
the reassurance and teaching of Alpha comes just at the right time. In
a world where film, video and even Internet information is preferred
to human interaction, Emmaus covers more than most.

What we discover is the age-old lesson: it is not possible to meet
people's needs in one complete book. There is no pre-determined
lesson plan for all types and abilities of groups of learners. People
who discover new friendships in discussion groups and the freedom
to roam into the real questions which interest them take responsibility for their own learning. They start with the questions which they
are asking for themselves – in spite of where a directive group leader
might want them to go. They bring their own histories and their
previous patterns of learning into the group. Once trust and human
warmth are established, people will offer their knowledge and styles
of learning in the service of the greater group task.

All of these contemporary ways of learning are good in parts. The
frustrating problem – or revelation – is that it is the learners, not the
providers, who will decide which good parts they want to take up or
offer for themselves.

'Faith on the Way' begins with that discovery – nothing momentous or earth-shattering. It is a response to the question about why we do not learn from our mistakes. We have all been to boring lectures: some of us have given them! Very many of us have been embarrassed by having to play silly games, some of which have stuck in our memories because of the experience rather than through its benefits. We have all been silent at one time or another in fear that we would look foolish if we spoke.

Equally, we have all felt a sense of achievement through getting something done that we really wanted to achieve. We have each grown by coming close to the very personal experiences of others. Very many more of us than for generations are willing to admit that there is a dimension to life which we would define for ourselves as 'spiritual'. When we are asked to tell, do or demonstrate something, we fall back on a method we have experienced ourselves as inappropriate or ineffectual. Can we learn from our mistakes? We have come to the conclusion that by adopting the basic catechumenal style of 'Faith on the Way', we can. In the following chapters, in very personal ways, we will describe what this method and style of working has meant to ourselves and very many others. We will offer you some of their comments and experiences. Because our story, which began by working in the Adult Catechumenate, is now more than 40 years old, we then want to set out in a final chapter how we have reflected on and learned from our own experience. By taking our own medicine we then want to go on and offer a 'template' for adult life, growth, spiritual development and learning which we might want to discover in any congregation where God's renewing Spirit is at work.

References

Craig, Yvonne, 'We did it my way: the role of experiential learning in six approaches to adult education and training', *British Journal of Theological Education*, vol. 6, no. 1 (Spring 1994).

General Synod Board of Education, *Tomorrow is Another Country* (GS Misc. 467, Church House Publishing, 1996).

The National Society with the Bible Society, *Emmaus: the Way of Faith* (1998).

Ozanne, Jayne, *Hopes and Dreams for a Future Church* (Archbishops' Council, Church House Publishing, 2000).

Notes

1   The Alpha courses are produced by HTB Publications with a Course Book and Manual plus five videos from 1993.

❦

WHAT IS 'FAITH ON THE WAY'?

T HIS CHAPTER IS WRITTEN particularly for those who are
leaders in their local church. It gives, we hope, enough of an
outline of what it means to be 'on the Way' for clergy and church
council members to begin the work of deciding whether to adopt this
way of accompanying adults on their journey into Christian faith
and in their preparation for Christian initiation. It ends with a worksheet offering suggestions to help a committee, a working party or
project group to look more deeply at some of the issues that could be
involved in their own community with the actual people who would
be concerned.

What actually happens?

Instead of the clergy being the only people who prepare adults for
membership or a return to the church, either one-to-one or in a
group of candidates, the 'Faith on the Way' process (often known as
the 'catechumenate') has a number of special features:

- The involvement of the whole of the Christian community. Lay
people act as sponsors of the new enquirers and often as group
leaders. People who belong to the church take an active part in
welcoming and sharing with enquirers and are themselves caught
up in the work of personal growth and change. It is a mutual
process.

- The central idea of travelling along a journey, as the name 'Faith
on the Way' suggests. It is not simply a matter of being told
things about Christianity. People, both members of the church
and enquirers, recognize that being 'on the Way' means taking a
good, long time; it means being open to God making a difference in people's lives; and this demands space to reflect both on

the experience of life's events, discerning God's purpose within them, and also on the challenges which come with hearing the Gospel.

- 'Faith on the Way' gives opportunities for a number of special acts of worship which mark the recognized stages along the journey. The first 'Enquiry' stage consists of quite open preparatory sessions leading up to a celebration which welcomes the enquirer as a learner in the way of Christ. The second stage of learning and growing ends with a liturgy celebrating God's call and the individual's response, in which those enquirers who are ready to go on towards baptism or confirmation or to a formal recommitment to their membership of the church are accepted as candidates for baptism, confirmation, reaffirmation or reception. The period immediately leading up to baptism or confirmation, the time of final preparation, is marked by special events and prayers on the theme of 'turning and seeing anew'. The peak celebration of the journey is the liturgy of baptism, which for some may be an actual water baptism, for others it may be confirmation or a reaffirmation. This is followed by a period of reflection and setting out on a life of Christian mission and ministry, when people continue to meet and reflect on what has taken place and what God is calling them to do.

From the grass roots

One local minister tells us a personal story:

I regard my introduction to this movement as one of the most exciting events in over forty years of ministry. First meeting it at a conference for In-Service Training Officers, I was particularly impressed by the way some churches made preparation for baptism and confirmation a parish activity, with the congregation involved in the special services.

I discussed the conference with a group of parishioners. There was a good deal of interest and I felt encouraged to take the matter further. We organized a residential parish weekend and discussed and prayed about the possibility of making the congregation responsible for the preparation of adults. We decided to make a start with three candidates who were seeking confirmation. We selected sponsors. Candidates and sponsors made a public commitment during the Parish Communion, when our intentions were explained to the congregation. Ten members agreed to share in the programme. These and the sponsors made up two groups meeting once a fortnight.

We decided to make a start in December and to admit candidates to Holy Communion the following Easter. This gave us Holy Week as a time of special preparation. Meetings were on Sunday evenings, lasted two hours, and were planned with the sponsors and helpers.

Before I left the parish we had three similar programmes with, to my joy, candidates from the first year becoming helpers in the following years. In the last year there were ten candidates and 45 helpers. In fact, a fair proportion of the congregation joined in. Since I left, the programme has continued and is now in its eighth year.

A tool for evangelism

Both clergy and lay people are becoming more aware about ways of sharing faith experience. We recognize that we have to be able to offer the Good News to adult men and women, to be open to new enquirers and to new ways of being the Church. 'Faith on the Way' offers a route by which the Christian community in a parish or some other institution can find a new and effective method of accompanying enquirers into faith in Christ, to membership of the Church, and to their part in the ministry of the people of God for the coming of his rule on earth.

It is a method that has its origin in the welcome and initiation ceremonies of the early Church and has been developed in different ways around the world over the past 50 years. What we write is based on practical experience and the evidence of people and parishes in a great variety of situations.

In the rest of the book we shall try to avoid using technical words, but in order to put things in context we ought to point out that the way of working with people on their journey into faith described in this book has various names. The title that we are going to use is 'Faith on the Way', or simply 'the Way' for short. The name is simply an extension of the report of a working party to the House of Bishops of the Church of England which was published in 1995 and which has influenced the work of the Liturgical Commission and those who are involved in evangelism and in adult education within the church. Other names are used. Anglicans often talk about the 'Adult Catechumenate' or simply 'the catechumenate'. The Roman Catholic Church has its Rite of Christian Initiation of Adults (usually referred to simply as RCIA). In its Book of Occasional Services the Episcopal Church in the USA has a section on 'Preparing Adults for Holy Baptism' which offers guidance for the catechumenate and a series of short liturgies.

This approach of coming to faith and joining the Christian Church draws heavily upon the practice of the early Church in the first couple of centuries. The followers of Jesus by then had formed a minority movement in a world of competing beliefs, a situation that is shared today by most Christians in the various countries of the world.

Our Church in our age

Adult men and women at different stages of their lives ask searching questions about the meaning and purpose of life, and of their own lives in particular. There are many different groups offering answers to these questions in the marketplace. But it is still the case that enquirers come to the churches in spite of the fact that in most mainstream churches the figures for actual attendance at services are low. In *The Tide is Running Out* (2000) Peter Brearley charts the decline in English church attendance like this:

In 1979, 5.4 million people in England attended church on an average Sunday. Ten years later in 1989 that number had become 4.7 million. Nine years later in 1998 that number had become 3.7 million. A 0.7 million drop in 10 years has been followed by a 1 million drop in 9 years, a 13% decline over 10 years and a 22% decline over 9 years.

This has been at a time when the population has been increasing, from 46 million in 1979 to nearly 50 million by 1998. This means that Sunday church attendance, in percentage terms has become:
- 11.7% attending church on an average Sunday in 1979;
- 9.9% attending church on an average Sunday in 1989; and
- 7.5% attending church on an average Sunday in 1998.

The picture is mixed. On the one hand, the Church often looks out of place in the society in which it is set; it may seem tired, isolated, perhaps even lost. On the other hand, it does appear to have something to share that many men and women want. The churches have recognized that there is a need for explicit mission to the people of our own day and our own country.

Although we write from an Anglican perspective, we hope this book will be of practical use to people of many denominations who approach the community of Christians for help and companionship on a journey that may end in full membership of the Body of Christ through the celebration of baptism or confirmation or some other sign of mature commitment to the faith and the Church of Jesus.

The catechumenate has for several decades been marked by strong ecumenical dialogue and co-operation. As Anglicans, we readily acknowledge that much of what we have to share in this book has come from modern Roman Catholic sources, but its roots lie deep in the shared Christian story of the early Church. And this process of growing in faith is a generally accepted part of all Christian bodies.

This 'Way' is about conversion, faith in Christ, baptism and church membership. Baptism is a sacrament which the vast majority of Christians celebrate and one in which most Christians accept the validity of other churches' ministry. We start from a common base. We recognize the activity of the Holy Spirit in a person, leading him or her towards God the Father through Jesus, to prayer and worship, and to a life lived in obedience to the love of God shown in his Son within a fellowship of people who share his mission in the world. All of this is shared by people in many different churches who exchange resources and support each other in God's one mission in the world.

Some historical background

At the heart of the process is what Christians believe about baptism as a sacrament of initiation into the new life of Jesus Christ, crucified and risen, and sign of commitment to the way of discipleship as a member of his Church, living in the power of the Holy Spirit. The movement of personal conversion, the deepening sense of belonging to a community, growth in understanding of that community's beliefs and the series of liturgical events which marks the stages of the journey mesh together as a way of being the Church in mission.

In the early centuries of the Christian Church, those who were in the first stages of their membership (known as 'catechumens' – people under instruction) were very carefully prepared for baptism. The Church then was a tiny minority movement, often subject to persecution by the state or other hostile factions. It was important that its members should be well prepared for the responsibilities, and the dangers, that being a member of the Christian community brought. Thus there was a time of preparation, often lasting several years, during which catechumens belonged to the family of the Church but not fully. They had joined but were not yet baptized, and they did not yet take part in the Eucharist.

This pattern of helping people into Christian life was in use for about two centuries in different forms in various places across the Mediterranean countries which made up the heart of the Roman Empire. In AD 313 the Emperor Constantine issued an edict legalizing Christianity, and within a short time it became the official religion of the Empire. This meant two things: first, there was no longer the same urgent need of courageous preparation for belonging to the Church; and second, there were lots more people wanting to join – especially when being baptized became a condition for jobs in the civil service or commissions in the army. So gradually the long and intense time of preparation fell out of use. The road to baptism became simpler, and baptism itself became more general.

Leap forward to the twentieth century and to Roman Catholic missions in Africa. Here French missionary priests were looking for ways to train converts from other religions in the Christian way. They found their answer in their studies of the early Church. There, embedded like a fossil in church history, was a tool waiting to be modernized and used. During and after the Second World War, leaders of the Church in France recognized that their nation was far from being a Christian country and launched the Mission to France. They too looked for ways to train the new Christians who were converted from among their own neighbours and found such ways in the experience of contemporary Africa and in that of the early Church.

The Second Vatican Council required that the catechumenate should be restored as part of the regular life of the Roman Catholic Church – not simply as a doctrinal preparation for baptism, but as 'a formation in the whole of Christian life and a sufficiently prolonged period of training'.

From the Anglican standpoint

Some Anglican clergy over the past 50 years looked to the Catholic Church in France as the community where it was easiest to have conversations across the denominational divide. In the 1940s there were many who acknowledged a debt to the inspiration of such books as Abbé Godin's *France Pagan?* and the efforts of the Mission de France in confronting the lack of interest in religion. This was a time when Christians in England had to come to terms with a similar situation in their own country. A Church of England report had been published in 1945 with a title in the same vein: *Towards the Conversion of England* (Publications Board of the Church Assembly, 1945). Anglicans also learned from the activities of the French catechumenate.

In the early 1970s there began a 'European Conference on the Catechumenate'. Originally it was centred largely on France and French-speaking countries, but over the years it has drawn together enthusiasts concerned to develop the method in countries throughout Western Europe. Almost from the start there has been an Anglican presence in this movement. The 1983 meeting was held in London under the joint auspices of Anglicans and Catholics. It was marked by a formal visit to the Archbishop of Canterbury at Lambeth Palace and a reception at Church House, Westminster, the centre of the General Synod of the Church of England.

Liturgies

The only official services for the initiation of adults in the Church of England are the baptism and confirmation liturgies in the *Book of Common Prayer* and in *Common Worship: Initiation Services*. The Liturgical Commission is presently working on prayers and forms of service for use at different points along the 'Way'. Their interim report was issued in 1998 (General Synod of the Church of England, 1998).

The Episcopal Church of the USA gives its guidelines and outline liturgies in the *Book of Occasional Services*. The Church in South Africa also has a rite for the making of a catechumen. The Anglican Church of Australia also has liturgies for the catechumenate.

Official statements

Some twenty years after the Second Vatican Council, the 1988 Anglican Lambeth Conference made an important recommendation in the section of its report dealing with mission and ministry under the heading 'Baptism':

Preparation
Just as we urge thorough preparation of parents for the baptism of an infant, so all the more we recommend thorough preparation of both candidates and sponsors at the baptism of an adult. Because it is entry into the missionary Body of Christ, baptism should lead, through the supportive fellowship of the Church, to a maturing process in the Spirit and to a sharing of Christ's ministry of service in the world. We note and commend a widespread interest in the revival of an adult Catechumenate and invite Provinces to consider the provision of guidelines for this. (Anglican Consultative Council, 1988)

In England the General Synod passed a motion at its February 1990 meeting:

That this synod requests the House of Bishops, in the light of issues raised in the Knaresborough Report, *On Communion before Confirmation*, to consider the case for reviving the catechumenate in order that adults, young people and infants may be associated with the Church, as a preliminary to Baptism, and for making provision for a draft order of service, whereby candidates would be admitted to such a catechumenate.

This was followed by the July 1991 General Synod resolution:

That this Synod . . . ask the House of Bishops in consultation with the Board of Education, Board of Mission and the Liturgical Commission to prepare a paper on patterns of nurture in faith, including the Catechumenate. (*On the Way* is the report which responded to this resolution.)

Also in 1991, the Anglican Liturgical Consultation, composed of representatives of provinces throughout the world, meeting in Toronto, made the recommendation: 'The Catechumenate is a model for preparation and formation for baptism. We recognise that its constituent liturgical rites may vary in different cultural circumstances.'

The 1998 *Common Worship: Initiation Services* (Church House Publishing, 1998) owe their shape both to a new appreciation of the ancient practice of the Church and also to fresh thinking about the nature of baptism as expressing the identity and call of the Christian community today.

The Liturgical Commission notes:

Increasingly people are coming to baptism as adults. *On the Way* (Church House Publishing, 1995), following the 1991 International Anglican Consultation at Toronto, proposes that such baptisms should be supported by what it calls a catechumenal process in which baptism is integrated within the journey to faith.

The catechumenal process begins with the welcome of individuals, the valuing of their story, the recognition of the work of God in their lives, the provision of sponsors to accompany their journey, and the engagement of the whole Christian community in both supporting them and learning from them. It seeks to promote personal formation of the new believer in four areas: formation in the Christian tradition as made available in the scriptures, development in personal prayer, incorporation in the worship of the church, and ministry in society, particularly to the powerless, the sick and all in need. (p. 198)

Personal and parish experience

Peter Ball writes:

I am enthusiastic about the subject of this book. I believe in 'Faith on the Way' for several reasons which cluster around my experience that it works and two beliefs I hold about its truth. First, I believe that it is true to the Gospel carried by the tradition of the Church to which I belong. Second, I believe that it is true also to the way men and women learn about the God of Jesus Christ and move, or are moved, to give their lives to his worship and service within the fellowship of his Church.

For nearly seventeen years I was Rector of St Nicholas, Shepperton. This is a parish in the south west of London, not far from Heathrow Airport. It is largely a residential area. The people who live there tend to work either in the centre of London or on its western edge, or in jobs connected with Heathrow.

Inspired by Jim Cranswick, an Australian priest who helped us, we gradually, over three years, moved into a new way of preparing adults for confirmation. Until then, it had been the responsibility of the clergy, myself or the curate to lead adult confirmation classes. The first change was to call in a small group of lay women and men who would act as guides to those preparing for confirmation. It was the start of a shared ministry in this area of the parish's work.

Initially I tended to ask people to work on a one-to-one basis, with an enquirer meeting with a church member over a period of several months. But a study leave which I spent visiting France, Switzerland and Belgium to look at methods of training lay leaders persuaded me that this was too restrictive. Being the Church is about building and being a community. I realized that our method was short-changing the newcomers. They were not being introduced into an important dimension of discipleship: community. Thus we moved from a one-to-one basis to small groups.

Within a year or two a pattern developed. When there were, say, three or four people who wanted to enter more deeply into the faith, perhaps definitely thinking about being baptized or confirmed, I would ask a couple of people to lead a group for them. Sometimes this would be a husband and wife, but by no means always. We found it was good to have two leaders, for they could help each other in preparing and reviewing the sessions, as well as providing variety in their approach. Along with the leaders and the enquirers there would be other people in the group. Sometimes members of the church would ask for a refresher course; sometimes I would have my eye on people as future group leaders. Such people would play an invaluable part in helping the new Christians on their journey, providing insight from their own experience as well as friendship and encouragement.

It was a while before we introduced any liturgical element. What first attracted me about the catechumenate was that it offered a very good pattern for adult Christian education. Later we began to experiment quite tentatively with little celebrations at the Parish Eucharist to welcome people at the beginning of their course and to pray with them as the time for their confirmation drew near. I have since moved on to see that the formation side and the liturgical side of the process are dependent on each other; they work together for the candidate's growth towards Christian maturity within the community.

I left Shepperton to become a Residentiary Canon at St Paul's Cathedral. Since I resigned from that post I now spend more time working with people from different churches and in different countries. I act as consultant to parishes as they begin to work along the lines outlined here. The approach of each parish varies, of course, with their different traditions and the different personalities involved; but I have been deeply impressed by the kind of testimony that all have given to the validity and genuineness both of the educational side of this 'Way' and of the celebrations they have held with candidates and the congregation of their church.

Summary outline

So, what is this 'Way' that we are so enthusiastic about? It is a way in which the Church accompanies men and women along the first stages of their journey into the Christian faith. For some this will lead to baptism, or the affirmation of their baptism in confirmation and Holy Communion, the sacrament that marks conversion and joining the community. For others it may be a question of renewing a commitment to a belief and membership that was formally marked when they were much younger.

The first mark of this 'Way' is *welcome*. It is an attitude that values the enquirer as the most important person in the process; that is marked by a real willingness to listen to her or him; and that respects the life stories which such enquirers bring, their interests, and the

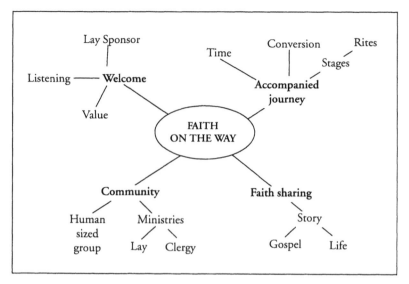

questions with which they come. The most obvious people to do this welcoming are the lay people of the church, and this ministry is expressed formally in the work of sponsors.

The second mark is *an accompanied journey into faith*. It has recognizable stages which can be celebrated in specially designed liturgies involving the congregation and the candidates.

Talk about a journey leads on to the third mark: this 'Way' is concerned with *sharing faith* in God through Jesus Christ and accompanying the process of conversion. It uses that language rather than the language of Christian instruction. We are dealing with personal change of direction and growth in faithfulness rather than the acquisition of knowledge about religion. This takes a longer time than is usually envisaged with present-day confirmation courses.

Fourth, experience has shown the great value of small groups as the place where new Christians can mature through experience of the community on a human scale. *Community* matters a great deal in this process. Candidates have come to join, or at least to test out, the community, the traditions it enshrines, and the message it has to share.

Members of the community can have many different ministries within the process. In particular, there is a variety of lay ministries which may seem to take over from the clergy much of what, in the past, they have considered their province. Lay leaders are responsible for accompanying and directing the enquirers in their groups.

The clergy can discover a new role as leaders of lay teams, exercising their calling as pastors and teachers in a fresh way through encouraging, training and enabling the members of the community to 'be the Church' in their own place.

Sponsors take on the role of friends and pastors to new Christians. The whole congregation is invited (or challenged) to accept responsibility for welcome, for support, and for the encouragement of their prayers.

Why change?

Over the years we have found that different sorts of people respond to different arguments for changing to this 'Way'. There is often, quite simply, a sense of dissatisfaction with what is happening at present, an awareness that adults are not getting all that they should from their confirmation classes. There are some who are encouraged by the evidence from other parishes and communities that this method works: that people who have gone through the process develop into mature Christians; that the quality of church life in the parish seems to deepen. There are others who are impressed by the Roman Catholic rite and by the way it has taken root in parishes.

In the final resort, though, it is only through personal experience and the experience of your own church that you can really measure the worth of what is on offer here. It is a case of 'Suck it and see'. That is why the worksheets are a built-in part of this book. If you do begin to adopt this 'Way', then please remember that you need to be part of the process of change. As the late James Dunning, one of the leading lights in the movement, said: 'The great commandment here is "Thou shalt not do unto others what thou hast not done for thyself".'

Parish stories

Here is a story from a vicar in a suburban parish:

> We had our confirmation on the night of Easter Eve with some sixteen adults being confirmed and some of them baptized. We had two groups, one led by lay people and one led by me and a lay person. They began in September and went on officially until the following September, but they still continue

unofficially as groups of friends meeting about once a month. It has been a wonderful year for leaders, candidates and sponsors; everyone has got such a lot from the experience.

Another group has now been formed under the leadership of two different lay people and we are planning for a confirmation on Whitsunday morning. The group is very mixed and we haven't yet moved to the point where they are to be introduced to the congregation and matched up with sponsors; some of them are sitting very delicately on the edge of the church and I am having to play it very carefully by ear.

This is just to say that we are continuing here at St Mary's and it is gently and gradually transforming the parish.

A lay leader from another parish writes:

The two cycles here had very different participants. The first year had a group of men and women in their sixties and seventies, the second a group in their middle to late twenties. We met for two and a half hours each Wednesday. After initial awkwardness and hesitancy for about two weeks, the commitment of both groups warmed to the feeling of community. The spirit was very much one of a voyage, an adventure, a journey, a pilgrimage into the unknown.

The unpredictable prospects of the weeks yet to come tended to draw us closer to each other. The younger group grew in maturity and conversely the older group grew more excitable and young again, as if years were falling off them and they could start life again. Humour and honesty flowed out. It was revealing to watch someone of sixty coming to learn about God for the first time who suddenly realizes that God had intervened in their life unbeknown to them perhaps some 30 years earlier. The younger people were more interested in 'technical' questions, picking passages of scripture apart to get the meanings out.

I admit to a feeling of great pleasure and satisfaction myself in being able to take part. They taught me just as much as I taught them. It was a great moment to go with them to the cathedral on their confirmation day.

Worksheet

Having read thus far, you may find it helpful to look at Worksheet 1. It is designed for those who have responsibility in the parish, and may raise questions to bear in mind as you read the next two chapters.

Worksheet 1

How to start
For the church council or committee who are deciding what to do about adults coming into the church.

Preparation
Read Chapters 1 and 2.

Task
The group should meet, perhaps more than once, with the following tasks:

1. Work through these questions and any others that come out of the discussions:
   (a) What is the current position in your church concerning adult enquirers? How does the church meet them? What is the quality of welcome? How many adults are confirmed? How are they prepared? What are your feelings and comments about what happens at present?
   (b) Having read about 'Faith on the Way', what does it offer to your church? How well would it suit your church?
   (c) If you believe your church should adopt this method, what are the decisions that have to be made?
   (d) Who should take those decisions?
   (e) What do you think are the main differences between what happens now and what 'Faith on the Way' offers? What changes would need to be made?

> (f) What problems have you already encountered and what problems do you anticipate?
> (g) How could you meet these problems?
> 2. Come to a formal decision as to whether to adopt or to recommend to the appropriate body that your church adopts 'Faith on the Way'.
> 3. If you decide in favour, arrange dates for two planning meetings.

References

Brearley, Peter, *The Tide is Running Out* (Christian Research, 2000), p. 27.

Common Worship: Initiation Services (Church House Publishing, 1998).

On the Way: Towards an Integrated Approach to Christian Initiation. GS Misc 444 (Church House Publishing, 1995).

Towards the Conversion of England: a plan dedicated to the memory of Archbishop William Temple. A report of a commission on evangelism appointed by the Archbishops of Canterbury and York pursuant to a resolution of the Church Assembly passed at the summer session, 1943 (The Press and Publications Board of the Church Assembly, 1945).

The Truth Shall Make You Free; the Lambeth Conference 1988; the Reports, Resolutions and Pastoral Letters from the Bishops (The Anglican Consultative Council, 1988).

THREE

A WELCOMING CHURCH

Who is this for?

This chapter is written particularly for the people who have to make decisions in the life of the local church – for those involved in planning and putting into action the changes that 'Faith on the Way' may mean in your particular place. The chapter contains a series of worksheets to help you earth the subject in your own situation and see what action needs to be taken.

The background

We live in a world that has seen 2,000 years of Christianity. In much of that time the culture of many countries around the world became Christian. In the United Kingdom the teaching of religion, and in particular the teaching of Christianity, has a special place in the state education system. There is a widespread layer of what is often called 'folk religion', which often lies beneath professed Christianity. However, as we saw in the last chapter, a rather harsher picture of the decline over decades in the practice of Christianity in Britain comes from surveys of church membership. George Gallup says 'The gulf between what we believe in our heads and what we feel in our hearts and practise in our lives is growing wider.'

If you are interested enough to read as far as this, it is probably because you recognize that even if this experience of overall decline in numbers is true in your own church, there are still newcomers who want to join, people who think Christianity may have something to offer them. So who are they?

They are likely come from anywhere on a wide scale of previous contacts with Christianity. Some people who discover a living and active faith as adults may well have met with Christianity and the

Church earlier in life. They have some kind of prehistory of faith or knowledge. There will be others for whom the teachings of Jesus or the fact of the Church are totally new.

We shall also meet people at different stages on the journey of sacramental initiation into the Church. The statistics for all churches show a dramatic decline over the last 30 years in the number of infants baptized compared with the number of babies born. The experience of most parishes is that we more often deal with adult preparation for confirmation of people who were christened as babies. There is, however, an increasing number of adult candidates for baptism.

This variety of people's experience and the wide range of their religious histories points to the need we shall encounter over and over again: to be adaptable in responding to people's circumstances, to new events, and changing situations.

What we need to emphasize and shall repeat again and again is that the main concern of 'Faith on the Way' is with people in the early stages of searching for a deeper faith. We hear regularly from leaders and helpers, as well as from parish clergy, about the wonderful effects that taking part in the programme has had on church life and on the individual discipleship of church members. But this is not the purpose of the scheme. 'Faith on the Way' is not a programme for parish renewal or for deepening the faith of church members, however much it may have those valuable consequences. It exists first and foremost for *enquirers*, for *newcomers to the Church*, for *candidates*. We are dealing with the work of accompanying people on a spiritual journey, especially in the early stages.

Why do people come?

As we look around the congregations we have served, we recognize that the events of family life often lead people towards the Church. When a baby is born, the parents want a christening. The feelings of joy and gratitude at the birth of a baby, coupled with the recognition of responsibility, often evoke some sort of religious response.

Children at primary school ask questions, or perhaps want to join Sunday School. Parents may feel they need more in the way of knowledge if they are to answer or support their son or daughter. Parishes that have a church school know the pressure there can be on places. Parents who originally come to church for ulterior motives may find that they stay out of conviction!

Preparing for a wedding may move a young couple to think more deeply about faith as they look forward to the prospect of their life together. For many it is their first experience of meeting the Church.

Illness, death and bereavement are part of the other side of life that brings people into contact with the Church. Most families still expect a religious funeral service in church or at the local crematorium. There may also be counselling available to help a person through grief.

There are other hurts, too. It may be the pain of marriage break-up or problems between parents and children; unemployment and debt; perhaps the weight of alcoholism or drug addiction; not to mention the many named or nameless fears, anxieties and depressions that darken so many lives.

Because of the speed and frequency with which people move round the country, many are lonely. They need to find a way to make friends. The local church can often provide an opportunity for meeting others through services or through clubs and organizations.

At some point in their journey through life, most human beings ask what it all means, what is the point of it all? This search for meaning and purpose in life brings many into contact with the Church.

Alongside these and the many other events in life that draw or push people towards the Church, there are people whose need is religious or spiritual. Quite simply, they sense a desire for God, and they want to know more about Jesus.

The Christian offer

The next thing is to ask how your church responds to these men and women who come with their expectations and demands, how it welcomes the gifts that they bring.

There's a saying, 'You don't get a second chance to make a first impression.' It should be written in big, bold letters on the walls of clergy vestries and at the head of the quarterly rotas of church-wardens, sidesmen and sideswomen, Sunday greeters and welcoming teams.

Try to put yourself in the shoes of a new enquirer coming to your

church and sense what he or she may experience. How would it strike
you? What words would you use: 'Friendly'? 'Warm'? 'Embarrass-
ing'? 'Scary'? 'Unwelcoming'?

We are talking here about first contacts, wedding bookings,
arrangements for a funeral after a tragic, pointless road accident, or
an enquiry about which day the Mothers and Toddlers group meets.
Look at the quality of welcome that marks out the life of your church
and the people who are its public face.

God loves

The infinite value of each child of God should be the mark of the way
Christians treat the people they meet. This is easily said, but very
much harder to put into practice.

People matter, and so does everything about them. We all have our
own story, our own background. Our social class is part of how we
approach the world around us. We are at home with the things we are
at home with: jobs and leisure activities; favourite television programmes and Sunday papers; sports or hobbies. We are at home with
the kind of people we get on with, too. And we are used to the way in
which we try to make sense of life in general – what in the broadest
sense can be called our faith.

Look first at the negative side. Ask whether the church to which
you belong devalues any of those aspects of a person's life and
surroundings. Who is unwelcome? It is a hard question to ask of a
Christian community, but it has to be faced. There are limits to what
any group can tolerate. Scandal, fears, snobbery, shyness, embarrassment and dislikes are things that are common to most people,
Christians included. Where do you and your friends at church draw
back from meeting people who upset or threaten you?

Look on the positive side, however, and see what welcome can
mean. The God we meet in Jesus Christ is a God who loves people.
He loves them as they are here and now. He also sees the full potential that they are capable of growing into with his help. He is a God
who forgives and heals. We call Jesus 'Our Saviour'. New Testament
writers occasionally used the same word for 'saving' and for 'healing'.
In the stories of Jesus meeting, healing and saving people there is a
constantly recurring theme of his acceptance and love meeting
people whose experience of life was one of rejection and dismissal.

Is your church one of those churches where people come for help and for healing of one sort or another? Do people find there what they are looking for? If they do, can you say how it happens?

Listen!

You may use the words 'evangelism' or 'evangelization' to describe the work of the Church and of individual Christians presenting the Gospel to people and accompanying them along the way that leads into Christian faith.

Anglicans and Free Church people are more likely to talk about 'evangelism'. For most people it means going to preach the Gospel to people who have not heard it. A territory has been evangelized if Christian missionaries have worked there. The main activity is speaking to others about the Gospel, and the agent of evangelism is the Christian and the Church.

The word 'evangelization' is more likely to be used by Catholics and tends to have a stronger content of conversion to it. For them, someone is evangelized who has not only heard the Gospel proclaimed, but has been moved to take it to heart. The process of evangelization is the process of presenting the Gospel and accompanying the hearer into faith. Here the agent is the Gospel and the Holy Spirit.

Whichever word you use, the work has to begin with welcome. The first step in evangelism must be respect for the other person. True evangelists are people with big ears and big hearts: they are not necessarily people with big mouths!

Welcome is vital for two reasons. Without it, newcomers are put off. They feel unwanted, they sense a lack of respect, and they have to be very brave or very determined to keep on coming back for what they need. They can just as easily go away. Welcome is also vital for the basic Christian reason that it reflects the way God deals with us. The Gospel is about God going out of his way to be with us, to give each human being the respect that is part of his love for her or for him.

A church that is effective in mission, which has taken to heart the call to evangelize, and within which people are able to learn, is a church whose members have learnt how to listen. This does not always come easily. It is a skill that most of us have to take the trouble to practise. It requires attitudes that run counter to much of the culture around us.

Listening demands a real respect for the other person and for their ideas, their character and their habits. It requires unselfishness in a culture that celebrates individual achievement and success above caring and generosity.

Listening is also a skill that can be improved through exercises. There should be opportunities for this near you. It is worth making the effort to develop your understanding of how you come across as a speaker and as a listener, how much 'body language' matters, and how you feel when you yourself are not being listened to properly.

The welcoming church

The obvious public occasion for judging the quality of your church's welcome is when someone new comes to a service. The questions concern the friendliness of the people who do the greeting at the door, the atmosphere of the congregation at worship, and what could be called the 'accessibility' of the whole occasion – how easy or diffi-cult it is to enter into what goes on. The same questions could be asked about a church social evening, badminton club or youth fellowship.

Telephones are a vitally important means of welcome in the modern world. How is the phone answered at your vicarage, pres-bytery, manse or parish office?

Alongside this official face of your church, there is another far more important (but less obvious) area for welcome. It is in the everyday contacts between church men and women and the people they meet as they go about their daily lives. These are the real mis-sionaries and it is their attitudes that matter as much as the official ones. Church people and their homes can be the key to effective welcome.

'Open spaces' round the church

This consideration of the quality of welcome leads on to thinking about the way a church organizes itself for welcome. Look at your own church and think about other churches you know; you may well recognize this sort of pattern:

- There is a core of committed church people; they are regular attenders; they provide money through stewardship or planned giving; they take responsibility for the leadership of different aspects of church life and for the management of its affairs.
- The less committed people are a larger group. There is no doubt that they belong. They are church attenders who take part in activities connected with the church, but they are not at the heart of things.
- There is a large number of occasional attenders. They would be extremely hurt to be told that they did not belong to their local church, because they think of themselves as members, even if the keener church people might question the depth of their commitment.
- Then there is the fringe. A great many people have connections with the church. Perhaps it is a childhood connection through Sunday School. We are forever amazed by the number of people, men in particular, who seem to think that they will get into heaven, or at least count as members of the church, on the strength of having played football with a great curate in the Youth Club!
- For many people it is something to do with family; their children are in the church school or are Cub Scouts and Brownies in the church pack. Churches often have clubs, day centres or playgroups in their halls and people come into contact with the church through these.

Thus there is a kind of 'open space' around the church, an uncommitted place where contacts with a low level of commitment can occur between men and women and the Christian community. It is here that most evangelism actually takes place, whether formally or in a quite informal way. It is a place of enquiry.

Time of enquiry

In this 'open space' round the church, people meet Christians and test out for themselves whether the community and the things it stands for are attractive. It is where most evangelism takes place. For most people it is not a formal stage in their approach to the church. There are no set ways by which people come, though there may be similarities. So there are no set ways for parishes to meet them.

There is a very wide variety of ways in which different church communities manage this stage of enquiry. Some parishes hold organized meetings for newcomers to get together with the church and to find out answers to their initial questions. Others begin very early to establish the preparation groups with sponsors and enquirers. Others, again, rely on the informal contacts between people and church members or the clergy.

Whatever method is adopted, this is a time for telling stories, talking about things that are important to us and learning about the lives of others. It is a time when the Church can hear the questions asked by enquirers. It is a time for simply getting to know people, learning where they come from, what their life is like, and where their interests lie. It is also a time for the first presentations of the message of the Church.

'Getting to know' is a two-way process. People have come to find out about Christianity and the Christian community in the local church. They want to test it out for themselves to see whether it offers an answer to their questions or a way of meeting their own particular needs. Sometimes they may need a good deal of help in recognizing and putting these needs into words. Many people have to be helped towards acknowledging their need for reconciliation with God.

The church person is in a position to share the Gospel with them: but sensitively. The leader of a group of enquirers is advised to keep a notebook in which to write down after each meeting just what the people were asking or saying about faith, putting it in the actual words they used. This is so that when it comes to responding with answers from the Gospel, he or she can use words and phrases that have come from the others and are part of their vocabulary. Listening matters as the first act in communication. In the communication of the Gospel that is evangelization, it is vitally important.

The lay person's ministry

The rest of this book is about how ordinary, regular worshippers can become better able to share the Christian faith with those who approach the church to discover what it stands for; to find answers to their questions; or to have their particular need met by the community which stands for the God who showed his love in the life, death and resurrection of Jesus Christ and who continues to show that love today.

The most important tool that the Church has in this work of evangelism is the people who make up its membership. That is why it matters so much that their strengths, their insights and their experience should be valued and developed. What is more, they have both the responsibility and the authority for exercising this ministry in their own baptism.

We keep coming back to sentences in the introduction to the Roman Catholic Rite of Christian Initiation of Adults:

> The people of God, as represented by the local Church, should understand and show by their concern that the initiation of adults is the responsibility of all the baptised. Therefore the community must always be fully prepared in the pursuit of its apostolic vocation to give help to those who are searching for Christ. In the various circumstances of daily life, even as in the apostolate, all the followers of Christ have the obligation of spreading the faith according to their abilities. (RCIA, 1987)

Gospel

The dialogue of evangelism may begin – very often does begin, and perhaps always should begin – with the Church listening to the enquirer. But it is a dialogue. The Church has its news to tell. The Christian has something to offer to meet the need, respond to the question, or awaken the awareness of the other person. You may notice that we swing between using 'Church' and 'Christian', between the organization and the individual. This is intentional. Both personal experience and collective experience are involved. There is the story that the Christian community has to tell. This tradition is carried in the Old and New Testaments with the stories of God's communities and the events that happened to them – and, above all, the story of Jesus. It continues in the churches to which we belong. As members of the community of faith, we have something bigger than ourselves to hand on to new people.

But we also have our own personal and individual story to tell and our own personal and individual faith to share. If you have read as far as this, we can assume you have some interest in the subject. You may not believe that your interest is worth a great deal. If we asked you to speak about your faith, you might well say that it was very weak and you'd rather not say anything. We respect your reticence, but we suggest you make the jump!

At the end of St Luke's gospel you will find the account of the two disciples walking to Emmaus on the first Easter evening and their meeting with the risen Jesus. It gives a remarkable example of this mixture of personal experience and the deep roots of tradition. There is both the disciples' eye-opening awareness that it is Jesus alive and with them, and their recognition of the immediacy and relevance of the scriptures that he opens to them. Their response is to rush back to the others and shout about their new faith (Luke 24:13–35).

Worksheet 2A: Are we a welcoming church?

For the same group as Worksheet 1.

Preparation
Read the section 'Why do people come?' on pages 36–7.

Task
1. Consider the people who have joined the church in the last year.
   (a) Who were they?
   (b) What have they said about their reasons for coming?
   (c) What attracted them?
   (d) What kind of background do they come from?
   (e) Did they have church contacts before?
2. How did you come into the Church? Tell each other in pairs or small groups and record your findings.
3. Answer the following questions:
   (a) How do people in your area get to know about your church?
   (b) What information is made available, and how?
   (c) Where would local people go if they wanted information?
   (d) How would they know where to go?
   (e) What are the points of contact for adults? For children?

Worksheet 2B: How we welcome

Preparation
Read the section 'The Christian offer' on pages 37–8.

Task
1. As a whole group, or in twos, threes or fours, answer these questions:
   (a) What kind of experience might someone have who telephoned the vicarage, presbytery or church office?
   (b) What kind of experience might they have if they knocked on the door of the vicarage, presbytery or church office?
   (c) . . . if they came along to a service?
   (d) . . . if they came to a meeting of a church organization?
2. List anything that might make people feel unwelcome.
   (a) Are there people you would be surprised to see in church?
   (b) Any particular age group?
   (c) Any particular type of person?
3. Are there ways in which your parish could do better at:
   (a) Publicity and informing people?
   (b) Getting into contact with people?
   (c) Welcoming newcomers?
   (d) Helping them to feel at home?
   (e) Accepting the unlikely people?
   (f) Listening to what people really have to say?

Worksheet 2C: The shape of your church

Preparation
Read the section '"Open spaces" round the church' on pages 40–1.

Task
Work through these questions together:

1. Do you recognize this description of a church? Is yours similar or different?
2. Who are in the core of committed church people?
3. Who do you know who attends church but is not at the centre of things?
4. Who comes occasionally?
5. Which people have links with the church but don't come to services?
6. What kinds of links are you aware of?

Worksheet 2D: Listening

Preparation
Read the section 'Time of enquiry' on pages 41–2.

Task
Either:

1. Working in pairs, try this imaginative exercise:
   One member of the pair is a church member. The other has come to church for the first time but wants to talk about what is on his or her mind (it may be a bereavement, a financial or family problem, concern to bring up a child properly, the baptism of a baby, or something joyful they want to share).
   Role-play the conversation between the two. Then review the conversation.

(a) What did the newcomer feel about the church person's welcome? . . . about the quality of listening?

(b) What can the church person remember and re-tell about the newcomer's concerns?

Or:

2. Another exercise in pairs:
Being yourselves, and not pretending or imagining anything, tell each other how you reached your personal faith.
Who inspired you? . . . taught you? . . . welcomed you? etc.
Then review the conversation.

(a) How were you listened to?

(b) What did it feel like to be the listener? Easy or hard?

(c) What did it feel like to be telling your story?

Reference

Rite of Christian Initiation of Adults; Approved for Use in the Dioceses of England and Wales, Scotland (Geoffrey Chapman, 1987).

FOUR

❧

COMPANIONS ALONG THE WAY

THIS CHAPTER IS ABOUT the ministry that companions or sponsors and other lay people engaged in 'Faith on the Way' are asked to undertake. It is about the central idea of a journey into the Christian faith which for some people leads to church membership. It closes with two worksheets. Worksheet 3A is for the group that has the responsibility for introducing 'Faith on the Way' in the parish. Worksheet 3B gives two session outlines for the preparation and training of people who are to be sponsors and group leaders.

Many people following 'the Way' will be preparing for confirmation. For others, the goal will be baptism. For some who were baptized and confirmed earlier in life it will be a way leading to a celebration that reaffirms their adult faith. Each person will be on a journey that is private and individual to them. Just as different people have a similar sort of skeleton, so there are likely to be similar elements in different people's journeys. The details vary, but there are elements common to all.

The journey starts with a spiritual search for something not yet expressed or with the early beginnings of personal belief in God and Jesus. It leads to a point where people can make a personal commitment of trust and belief and become active members of the church. The journey also, of course, carries the possibility that people may decide not to continue and to opt out.

Journey language

Speaking about a journey marks something of a change from much established church practice where talk of confirmation *classes* tends to give echoes of school and education. For most ordinary people this means being told about things. There are teachers and there are pupils: people who know and ignorant people needing to be taught.

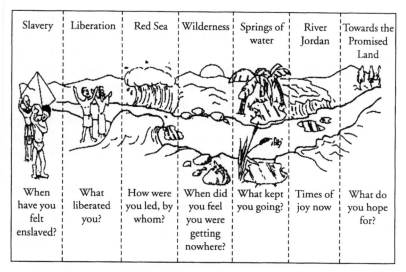

Slavery	Liberation	Red Sea	Wilderness	Springs of water	River Jordan	Towards the Promised Land
When have you felt enslaved?	What liberated you?	How were you led, by whom?	When did you feel you were getting nowhere?	What kept you going?	Times of joy now	What do you hope for?

Journey in faith. From *Telling the Story, Sharing the Faith* (Home Mission Committee of the General Synod Board of Mission and Unity).

For many adults these images and phrases immediately call up a sense of inadequacy and failure. It is sad but true that grown men and women can feel threatened by the idea of learning.

When we talk about an accompanied journey, we are offering a different image. We are talking about travelling along a road with a companion who is there not as a teacher but as a guide. It is walking with a friend who has already travelled their own road and knows some of the features of yours.

Journey also implies movement and change. Certainly there is knowledge to be shared and there will be questions to face, but the real work is in the many-sided personal changes that are conversion to Christ. You start from where you are and move on through each successive point on the road to the place which feels like home.

It sounds simple, but each part of that last sentence is very important. You can only begin where you are. For the companion, this is a matter of listening sufficiently carefully to discern what their friend's present position is, what they believe, what they find difficult. They need to listen in order to understand the questions and what lies behind them.

Where people are is their present gift from God. Church people can easily fall into the danger of being so full of the truth which they believe God has given them that they simply have to tell it first, before listening to the other person. It is no bad thing to remember that God has been there already; is there already. We do not bring God to the new Christian. Our job is to help the enquirers to see where God is at work in their lives and in their hearts.

The idea of journey takes in much more than simply learning with your mind about Christianity and the Church. It is about entering into a relationship with God that changes the way you live. It has a bearing upon your understanding, your feelings, your experience of life, your attitudes and the choices you make.

The shift is from instruction to conversion. It is about how people make changes (are changed), how they respond to new experiences and relationships, as they enter into new awareness of the Christian faith and the Christian community. It is about growing towards maturity as a disciple of Jesus.

How long?

Time is another area where you may find differences from what has been the accepted practice of your church. A course of preparation for confirmation might be expected to run for about two or three months. During that time people would have sessions on the main teachings of the Church. It is possible that they may follow a course laid down in a handbook. The assumption is that they will be ready for confirmation when they have finished the course. They will be reckoned to know enough.

In 'Faith on the Way', *knowing enough* is certainly important, but the signs of conversion are vital. What matters is a deepening relationship with and commitment to God as known in and through Jesus Christ. This will show itself in an altered pattern of life as someone comes to accept that the way they believe affects their everyday behaviour. Once you accept that, you move into a different time-scale. The pattern of acquiring knowledge through attendance at classes switches to one of personal change. This is a far slower process. It deals with attitudes, relationships and things of the Spirit. The rhythm is far more leisurely than that of head-knowledge. Instead of a couple of months, we can be looking at a journey that may take a year or more.

To change the pattern of confirmation preparation like this may

seem something of a threat. Candidates may feel impatient, especially when their friends went through the process much faster last
year. The clergy may feel they are asking too much. But the best witnesses for this extended time are the candidates themselves. People
who have been given the space to grow and mature through 'the Way'
tend to feel very sorry for the others who rushed the job under the
old system.

Commonly, groups will meet for most of the church's working
season, which starts when the schools go back after the summer
holidays and leads up to Easter. This would be particularly the case in
the churches where the Easter Vigil is the time for baptism and confirmation. For some people it may be right to think of a period that is
a great deal longer. For others it may be shorter. Programmes, calen-
dars and timetables are convenient tools in all this, but they should
never be allowed to become straitjackets.

Accompanied

In his *Finding Faith Today* (1992) John Finney gives the findings of a
survey of over 500 people who had made an adult profession of faith
in the past twelve months. The profession event could be confirmation or reception into membership of a church; adult baptism; the
Rite of Christian Initiation of Adults; or some other public declara-
tion. Several points in the book concern us here. Almost two-thirds
of the people described their process as a gradual rather than a
sudden one. The three major factors which helped them on their way
to faith were their spouse or partner, Christian friends, and a minister
of the church. God uses the ordinary people who are at hand to
accompany men and women into Christian faith. 'Faith on the Way'
seeks to learn from this practical experience.

This is because when most Christians tell the story of how they
came to the Christian faith or joined their church, they talk about
friends, the men and women through whom they began to discover
God in Jesus, and the fellowship of the community of believers. Only
a minority will talk about doctrines and statements about belief. The
way Christian faith is described and handed on in words is important, but for the vast majority of enquirers and new believers what
matters most is relationships – other people. Ask them what it was
that attracted them and held their interest and you will hear about

welcome, acceptance, friendship, warmth, inspiration and example.

We recognize these different kinds of experience and build on them. People approaching the faith or the Church need companionship. This is best given by lay members of the church. Various words are used to describe the more experienced Christian friends who accompany enquirers. Some churches talk of 'sponsors', others simply say 'companions'.

Sponsors stand as representatives of the church. So it is usual for them to be invited by the parish clergy. It may happen that an enquirer has in mind someone they would particularly like to choose as their companion, but it is always important that their choice is endorsed by the church. On the whole, it is probably best not to have a member of the enquirer's own family as a sponsor.

There are several different ways in which parishes use sponsors. Some have a one-to-one link between an enquirer and his or her sponsor. Sponsors take a full part in the group meetings with their enquirer, as well as spending time with them privately.

In others, the companions may not be members of the group that meets regularly to work with the candidates, but will have an important role to play in talking through afterwards what has come up in the meetings.

There are also parishes that do not work with one-to-one sponsoring, but rather see the group as the context in which the support and befriending take place. In this case, a group would be made up of enquirers and church people together.

We shall be dealing more fully with how these groups might work in the next two chapters. For the present we simply want to note how important they are for someone who is making their way along the faith journey. The meetings, the way people enter into conversation about things that matter deeply to them, and the friendships that grow over the weeks and months are a vital element.

Conversion

Conversion is about changing direction. A convert is a person who has turned or been turned. This makes it a very good family of words to use when we talk about a journey into faith. Along that journey there are plenty of moments when decisions have to be made. There is the first decision to start on the journey at all, a conscious choice to turn away from a life without God in order to seek him and his meaning for oneself. It is a process of personal change. There are many ways of describing it: growing in Christlikeness, being conformed to the image of Christ, or developing into the person that God has designed you to become.

In this change Christians have always recognized that there is a dialogue going on. Conversion is something that God effects in a person's life: it is God's initiative. On the other hand, the human person is not simply a passive object. We have been given a power of choice. Conversion is something in which each man and woman is involved. We can respond with a 'Yes' or a 'No' to God's initiative. In conversion, God turns us, changes our direction. But we also have a responsibility of our own to choose to turn in that new direction.

There is a variety of kinds of conversion in the New Testament. It's not all Paul-on-the-road-to-Damascus, by any means. His sudden blinding awareness of Jesus Christ and of his own need to respond to him has been repeated in the lives of people throughout the ages, but that is by no means the only pattern of conversion. Consider, for example, the calling of Andrew, Peter, James and John from their work as fishermen, or the friendship of Mary and Martha with Jesus. Each of them grew in making a faithful response to Jesus, but in different ways. These ways give us different pictures of conversion.

Step by step and stage by stage

Everyone's journey into Christian faith is different. It is personal and affected by all sorts of individual characteristics and outward circumstances. But most people can recognize that they have aspects in common with one another. 'Faith on the Way' recognizes these common points and celebrates them in the liturgical rites which it offers at different moments.

'Faith on the Way' really begins when someone moves from the stage of checking out the Church, from sniffing round what it has to offer, to some kind of request for deepening faith, more understanding or closer membership.

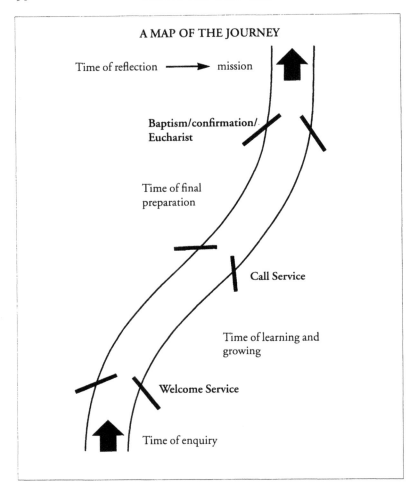

A MAP OF THE JOURNEY

Time of reflection ⟶ mission

Baptism/confirmation/
Eucharist

Time of final
preparation

Call Service

Time of learning and
growing

Welcome Service

Time of enquiry

Stories

Think of people like Fred, who nursed his wife for seven months at home before she died. His first real contact with the Church came over her funeral, when he found that the care he received was a great help. He had made friends at the Royal British Legion Club since he retired, but there was something about the service in church and the friendship that he began to experience from the minister and one of the men in the church which seemed to touch him at a deeper level than he found in the Club. Somehow he felt he wanted to get a little closer to whatever it was that seemed to help in his grief.

Kathy had never been christened, so when she came with Tim to arrange to get married at St Stephen's she was really very nervous. She didn't know if she could have a church wedding if she wasn't baptized. When the curate said she could still be baptized, even though she was an adult, she agreed that it would be a good idea, and decided to join the classes. Tim did, too.

Bernard was a successful businessman. Over the years he had made a good deal of money. He and his wife had a nice house in the suburbs and a holiday home in the country. The children had completed their education and were living away from home. But what was it all for? Nice to be a two-car, two-home husband and wife, but what really was the point of life?

Cynthia had been away for a short holiday in Yorkshire. Early one morning she and her friend visited York Minster. It was quiet with not many people about, just somebody softly playing the organ. She felt something happen to her that she couldn't really explain. She knew it was true and lovely and real. It felt very good. It was like wanting something very much and getting it at the same time, but not being able to explain it. If this was God, she wanted more.

There are as many stories as there are people. There is a point where a person, faced with something like one of these experiences, makes a move towards the Church. They might speak with a Christian friend or turn up at church. They might even pick up the phone to make an appointment to see the minister. In one way or another, they make a definite first enquiring step on the journey.

The journey that different people travel in the Christian faith, the journey of conversion, has recognizably different phases and periods of developing growth and discovery. 'Faith on the Way' provides for these changes from one period or phase to another to be marked by special liturgies or rites. Some of these can be celebrated in church at the main Sunday service; others can take place in the regular meetings of the groups.

Service of Welcome

There comes a time in the faith journey when people recognize that they can no longer sit on the edge: they have either to walk away or to jump in. The time of enquiry in the 'open spaces' surrounding the church leads in due course to a moment of choice and decision. For some people it is a movement of the Spirit within themselves. They 'know' they must do something about it. For others, the pressure comes from other people or from outside events.

'Faith on the Way' starts when a group of enquirers and sponsors or helpers is formed and the members begin their journey together. This beginning can be celebrated in church. After a few weeks of group meetings one young woman said, 'Is there anything to show we've started?' In a liturgy such as this she could experience just that.

The Service of Welcome celebrates a desire to find out about the Christian faith. The commitment is to a search; it is not yet a commitment to formal membership or to baptism or confirmation. That may be the final outcome, but for most people it is more a matter of 'I want to go a bit further before I decide. I need to know some more, be more convinced that it's right for me.' It is also a celebration for the congregation to recognize what it means to be a Christian community ready to welcome new members and to accept responsibility for them. The church is aware that the enquirers are just taking early steps along a way that may lead them to full membership and that they will need help.

You will see outlines for the rite in Chapter 9. It is designed to do several things:

- The enquirers are taking an important first step at the beginning of faith and commitment. They are turning towards God and the life of a Christian. They are asking something of the Christian community, their local church. This service gives formal expression to where they are in their journey of faith. It can be seen as the first formal step on the road to – or, perhaps more exactly, as the first step of the staged process of – baptism itself.
- In this service the local church welcomes the new people and accepts their commitment to explore faith and membership. The sponsors who accompany them need to be seen to have a ministry within the church, so this could be the occasion for them to be commissioned.
- The rite is not centred only on people and the local community. It is also a time for prayer and for God's blessing expressed in giving the enquirers the sign of the cross.
- The local church meets to recognize the new enquirers; it joins in prayer with and for them. The witness of the new people who

want to join their community can often challenge regular church-goers to look again at the way they live out their own beliefs.

Learning and growing time

The Service of Welcome celebrates a first commitment to the Church and to a journey of learning and growing in the faith of Jesus Christ. It is like being engaged. It is not yet a full membership, but it is a belonging rather than a standing outside looking in. It leads into the period during which the enquirers and the people who are accompanying them get down to hearing the story of the Christian Gospel and relating that to the realities of their own lives and their own situations. We shall look more closely at this sharing of faith in Chapters 5 and 6.

Different people will take different amounts of time over this. Ideally the length of a course and what it contains should be tailored to fit every individual, because the enquirer is the central person in all that 'Faith on the Way' stands for. However, life rarely allows for that and adjustments have to be made so that as many as possible can travel together.

God who calls

The tradition that Easter is the great time for baptism goes right back to the early Church. St Paul, writing in Romans 6, clearly links baptism to Jesus' death and resurrection. There is a dying to an old way of life without faith, and a being born, or rising from death, into a new life in Christ. In the Church's year there are other special days that are also particularly suitable for baptizing people. The season of Epiphany celebrates the baptism of Jesus himself; Whitsun recalls the gift of the Holy Spirit to the Church and the baptism of those who responded to the preaching of Peter at Pentecost; All Saints is the time for remembering fellowship with all the faithful who over the centuries have been baptized into Christ.

Before a man or woman is baptized or confirmed, choices have to be made. Both the candidate and the local church need to be sure that this is the right step for them to be taking at this particular time. It may not be: he or she may not be ready yet to make such a commitment.

There are several people involved in discerning their readiness. There are the candidates themselves, those who accompany them, and the parish clergy. In the early Church it would have been the bishop who made the final decision whether or not to admit this person to the Church through baptism, and the bishop still has an important role to play today in the process of initiation.

This acceptance of the readiness of people for initiation can be celebrated in a service that is centred on the theme of God's Call. The focus of the liturgy is on the God who called Abraham, and who called Moses, the God who chose the holy nation. It looks to Jesus who called his disciples and invited them to be with him before he sent them out to be his messengers. It proclaims the same God who through baptism and the Eucharist calls men and women today to be 'a chosen race, a royal priesthood, a dedicated nation, a people claimed by God for his own, to proclaim the glorious deeds of him who has called you out of darkness into his marvellous light' (1 Peter 2:9).

Chapter 9 outlines the service of God's Call. The people who have spent time growing in the Christian faith, in their understanding of what it means to belong to the Church and in their awareness of the demands of their new faith upon their ordinary life and service of others, are now commended by their sponsors and other people in the Church to be baptized or confirmed at the celebration in a few weeks' time.

Period of spiritual preparation

The season of Lent was originally the time when candidates made their final spiritual preparation in prayer and fasting before their baptism at Easter. Whether or not the baptism or the confirmation in your church takes place at Easter, there should be some kind of special preparation for the candidates. The early Christians called it a time of 'enlightenment'. Just as Jesus withdrew from the busy-ness of his ministry to pray in the mountains before times of important decisions or special work, so this can be a time for particular emphasis on prayer. Themes may well include recognizing the challenges that the coming commitment presents to each person, and also recognizing their need for penitence and healing.

There are special services of prayer that can be used with the candidates in the preparation group or in the Sunday services.

Baptism and confirmation

When an adult is baptized, the liturgy shows very clearly how Jesus' death and resurrection are intimately linked with the change taking place in an individual. People die to a life lived without faith and outside the Church. They are born into a new life of faith, joining the community of Christians in the Church. They receive the sign of water and laying-on of hands; perhaps they are anointed with oil. They join with the church for the first time to receive the bread and the wine of the Eucharist in Holy Communion. In confirmation, people who were baptized earlier in life celebrate the truth and power of that baptism and receive blessing and grace for their life in the service of Christ in the world.

Reflection and ministry after baptism and confirmation

The time after baptism (traditionally the time between Easter and the feast of Pentecost) is the period for helping people to reflect on what has happened and to enter into the meaning of baptism, confirmation and Holy Communion for them. In the early Church it was a time for concentrated instruction by the bishop.

Many parishes bemoan the way young people disappear from church almost as soon as they have been confirmed. Often this is because they have seen confirmation like an exam to be prepared for, passed, and then forgotten – very different from 'the Way' offered here. We are dealing with preparation for the lifelong ministry of the baptized as Christians in the world.

Someone who is baptized is caught up in God's mission to his world. He or she becomes an agent in the work of the Kingdom of God which Jesus came to proclaim and initiate.

So this time after the great events of baptism, confirmation and first communion, or after a reaffirmation of commitment to baptism, is a very important opportunity for two aspects of the process. First, it is a time to reflect quietly and deeply on the spiritual and practical effect of what has taken place. Second, it is a time to relate all this to the opportunities for Christian witness and service that exist in everyone's everyday lives. The great themes of peace, justice and service of the poor will naturally have been part of the work of the main time of learning and growing in preparation for baptism or confirmation. But there is a sense in which the commitment carried in that sacrament casts a new light on people's involvement in them. Before, they may have looked at these themes almost from the outside; now they are to be part of their life.

It is a very important time, which ought never to be skimped. People rightly expect help from the church as they begin life as full members.

Variations

It is by no means common practice for all adults to be baptized or confirmed at Easter. Nor is it very common for adults who come to join the life of the local church to be unbaptized or even unconfirmed. The journey we have outlined in this chapter follows someone who is coming from a position of little or no faith. It celebrates their journey of conversion with celebrations that mark the stages along the way. It may lead to baptism, confirmation, a return to communion, or a renewal of baptismal promises.

In most parishes you will need to make your own adjustments to the basic pattern, because people are different and circumstances vary. The timetable may have to be fitted in with the bishop's availability for the confirmation service. The liturgies will almost certainly have to celebrate different sorts of sacramental journey for people who were christened as babies, people who were confirmed in adolescence, and people who are, as adults, following the path towards baptism.

It is important that the truth of people's journeys is respected in what happens in the services. It would be quite wrong in the liturgy to treat people who are baptized as if they were unbaptized, for instance.

The liturgies should express two sorts of truth. They need to be true to the personal lives of the candidates, celebrating the events of their discovery of Christian faith and their approach to the Church. They should reinforce their growing sense of commitment to the Christian way of life. They also need to be true to the wider tradition of the community the candidates are joining. In all this, it is really important to remember that just as the work of the group has to be adapted to the needs of its members, so the liturgies need to be adapted to express and celebrate the realities of the local circumstances.

Initiation is the whole process

It needs to be said quite firmly that what takes place in the different liturgies along the way is not an extended preparation for baptism. It is not as though the months spent learning and growing end with a first experience of the sacraments of initiation. Rather, the initiation is what is happening all through those months. What it celebrates is a person's conversion.

People discover the teaching of the Church. They grow in a relationship with God through Jesus in the fellowship of the Holy Spirit. They get to know some of the people in the church; they also begin to share in some of its worship and community life. They become aware that the faith they are entering into makes demands on the way they live and on the kind of choices they make in different aspects of their life. These things are not a preparation for initiation into faith and membership of the Church; they are stages in the actual process of initiation and they are celebrated in the stage-by-stage liturgy.

A sign of this unity in the rite is the marking of people with the cross. In the baptism liturgy of *Common Worship: Initiation Services* the signing with the cross comes as a response to the candidates turning to Christ, repenting of their sins, and renouncing evil. This is all that remains in our liturgy as at present authorized of the Rite of Entry (Service of Welcome) leading to the months of learning and deepening conversion. In *Common Worship* it is followed by the baptism in water within a couple of minutes.

The liturgy of 'Faith on the Way' is not stretching out a rite that was always short. Rather, it is recovering an ancient, extended ritual that, over the years, has become compressed into one single service.

(There are similarities with the marriage service. In the *Book of Common Prayer* the couple are asked to 'plight their troth', which is old-fashioned language for 'become engaged', and then immediately go on to exchange the consents which constitute their marriage. What was in earlier centuries a series of celebrations marking stages in the progress of two people towards marriage has been squeezed together into one liturgy.)

Worksheet 3A

Planning
For the group that is to be responsible for implementing and overseeing the process of 'On the Way' in the parish. It could be a committee of the church council or a specially formed task group.

Preparation
Read Chapter 4 (and Chapters 1 to 3, if you have not already done so).

Task
There are four main items of work. It may take two sessions to complete them.

1. Review: What has happened since the last meeting? What decisions have been taken by the relevant bodies in your church? Are you ready to proceed?
2. You have agreed to start 'Faith on the Way'. Who are the actual people you will be accompanying on their journey?
   (a) Is there already someone asking about confirmation? Are there people on the fringes of church membership that you should be inviting to join?
   (b) Are there church leaders, clergy and others you should ask for names of possible candidates?
   (c) What groups or individuals should you contact for possible people?
   (d) Should you advertise that the process is beginning? How? In the church magazine? Give it out in church? On the notice board, in the local press, on local radio?
3. The team: Who have you in mind as possible group leaders and sponsors? What part do you expect the clergy to play? What training do leaders and sponsors need before they begin?
4. What pattern of group working seems most appropriate for your place? What part do you expect the sponsors to play in the groups? Do you want to link sponsors one-to-

one with candidates or not? (See the section 'Accompanied' on pp. 51–2.)

5. Timetable: Should you make diary dates, pencilling in:
   (a) Training sessions for team members?
   (b) First meeting of the group(s)?
   (c) Possible date for a Service of Welcome?
   (d) Possible date for the Service of God's Call?
   (e) Possible date for baptism and confirmation?
6. What about the place of the bishop in the process? What consultations need to take place with the bishop about dates, etc.?

Worksheet 3B:
Training Session(s) for Sponsors

This is an outline of a basic preparation for sponsors. People who are to be group leaders should also take part.

The material that follows will take two sessions to complete. It could be a Saturday morning and afternoon, for instance, or two evenings.

Preparation
Read this book (or at least Chapters 1 to 4). As you read, be aware of and perhaps jot down in a notebook:

1. Bits of your own story that come to mind; the people and events that seem important to you.
2. Things in the book that excite you.
3. Things in the book that worry you or you don't agree with.

Task
1. The leader welcomes the members and invites them to say who they are and a little about themselves.

2. The leader introduces the session as a time for people to begin the work of accompanying someone on a journey of faith, making it clear that people are not under pressure to be more open than they feel is right for them and that the meeting is to be regarded as confidential.

3. Think for some minutes about why you are here, what you hope to get from the session(s), and what you think you have to offer to the session(s).

4. Depending on the number in the group, either share (3) with the whole group or split into more intimate small groups for this. Reflect on how this exercise feels (without moral judgement!).

5. Ask everyone to spend twenty minutes working in some way on their own story. Possible ways of doing this include:

   (a) Draw a 'life line' which shows the ups and downs at various ages of your life as you think of events that have been important.

   (b) List the people and the events that have mattered to you at different periods of your life. Note how you felt or feel about those periods. The 'Life Chart' on page 66 can be used as a model for this.

   (c) Draw a picture or make a diagram of your life now. (No artistic skill is needed!)

   (d) Make a cross dividing a page into four blocks and in the blocks list: what you enjoy, what gives you pleasure, what you dislike, what hurts you, what frightens you, what you hope for.

   (e) Think about the past week and reflect on a high point, something that has been good, and a low point, something that has been bad, for you.

   (This is a good point to make the break between sessions.)

6. Spend at least twenty minutes in pairs to share with each other the story you have been working on. Some pairs may want to divide the time in half, as listener and speaker and *vice versa*.

7. The whole group reviews the last two exercises. Look at questions like:

   (a) How do you feel about what has happened in the last hour?

   (b) What was it like to listen and to be listened to?

   (c) What stories of faith were there among the life stories?

8. Which of the activities you have just done would be suitable to do in a group with the enquirers?

   (a) Why or why not?

   (b) What do you think would be similar or different with them?

   (c) Look at the similarities and differences you expect. What skills and weaknesses have you seen in yourself and each other during this session?

9. Consider whether there is a need for further preparation sessions for sponsors or whether it is better for them to begin work and then come back for a reflection and 'in-service' training meeting.

Practicalities

1. Tell the sponsors who the enquirers are likely to be. See if they know them. Ask for prayers for them.

2. Consider how available people are to give time as sponsors, recognizing the commitment to meet with their enquirer and join in group sessions.

3. What are the practical arrangements that have to be made?

4. What are the important dates to be put into diaries for such events as first meeting of the group with enquirers, the Service of Welcome and planning meetings for that, and 'review sessions' for the sponsors?

Date	Events	People	Feelings or colour	Choices or call and response	Images of God

Life chart

Reference

Finney, John, *Finding Faith Today: How does it Happen?* (Swindon, British and Foreign Bible Society, 1992).

FIVE

WORKING IN GROUPS

THIS CHAPTER DEALS WITH the basic building block of 'Faith on the Way', the community in which most of the work takes place, a small group made up of enquirers and Christian helpers together. We hope that it will be particularly useful for people who are to lead groups or act as sponsors within them. Worksheet 4B on page 95 is primarily about training sponsors, though people preparing to lead groups should take part in the sessions. There is a set of worksheets on the training of group leaders at the end of Chapter 6 .

Working in groups

The vicar of a parish that has followed 'the Way' for several years writes:

> As I see it, the process is so much part of how things are done here and of the ethos of our Christian life that it hardly needs naming. In particular, there is an emphasis on working in groups in people's homes, including the confirmation preparation for adults and for young people. The other day we started yet another group for half-a-dozen enquirers. They are all led by members of the congregation, with the clergy only turning up when invited. Within such a group the participants set their own agenda, starting with their own concerns. We hope that the group will be flexible enough to respond to any pressing problem that any member needs to share. It's not chained to its programme. It would now be totally foreign to us to 'Teach the Faith' in a dogmatic, take-it-or-leave-it way.

Christianity as community

To become a Christian on your own is, if not impossible, at least very difficult and incredibly rare. You need other people. This is because Christianity is about sharing ideas and giving support in community. It involves belonging to a local congregation. Jesus did not leave behind him a religion: he left a group of people. Christians today are the successors of his friends and followers, the apostles and the others who made up the first body of disciples. 'The Body of Christ' is a fellowship that stretches back over the centuries and includes people of all continents. Jesus lives and works in the world through his people. That is why 'community' is one of the essential marks of this way of accompanying men and women into faith.

A central part of the process is that it involves the whole Christian community in the journey of baptism. It means meeting people at the beginning of their journey and praying for them while they are in their 'Faith on the Way' groups. Praying and working together as a community means that, when the time for the baptism or confirmation service comes, the words are much more real than responses from a book – however well these might be meant. As the introduction to *Common Worship: Initiation Services* says:

> The celebration of baptism should not be seen in isolation from the journey to faith in Christ. This journey is itself a process of discovery and transformation within a community. A baptism service must therefore help candidate and congregation discover each other as partners within a common adventure of faith. (Church House Publishing, 1998)

Special purpose

It is important to remember from the start that the groups come together in order to accompany men and women on their early steps of the journey into faith. They need to be formed for that purpose. Experience has shown that it does not work to use groups that already exist, like home groups or Lent groups, and adapt them for welcoming new Christians: the dynamics are all wrong. Preparation groups have a life of their own, a purpose of their own, and a time limit as well. They should last for as long as they are needed by the candidates and then stop meeting. They will have a continuing life as a group of friends who care for one another, but their official job is done once the new Christians are established in their new life and ministry.

Forming a group

How you go about setting up a group or groups will depend on the particular circumstances in your place. It will usually fall to the clergy to be responsible for this aspect of the work. It is often they who have the best awareness of who is who in the congregation and an insight into the suitable matching of candidate to helper. This task could also be shared with lay people who will be responsible for the group.

Experience has shown that the best practice is to consider the enquirers and see who in the congregation would be suitable as a leader for these men and women. Two leaders in a group are often better than one. A man and a woman working together provide a balance that often reflects the make-up of the group.

If there are four or five people who have asked to join the group with a view to being confirmed, think of two people who would be suitable leaders of a group to accompany them. Then look for people from the church who you might invite to join as helpers in the group. They might be people who have asked for a refresher course or people who you have selected as suitable for this specific group. They may also be people who themselves might be asked to be leaders of a group next year. What happens in this model is that the group travels together and provides support and care from within its own membership. The members act as companions to one another, although there is no formal one-to-one pairing of companion and candidate.

A second way of setting up groups begins with just such a one-to-one pairing. It is then a matter of forming a group from pairs of candidates and companions with leaders.

In a third pattern the group will consist of the leader or leaders usually meeting with the candidates alone. The candidates will have individual companions and will each meet with them at a different time to talk about their learning and growing in the faith, perhaps delving more deeply into things that the group meetings have dealt with. There will also be times when the companions take part in the main group meetings together with the candidates. This way of working has the advantage of asking the companions for a rather less demanding commitment as far as time is concerned. But there are drawbacks. When they are not part of the main work of the group, it is often difficult for them to know quite what they are supposed to be doing. It is easy for them to feel out of the main stream. There is also an opportunity lost. Time and again companions have said something like 'I don't know what Barry and Liz got out of this past year, but my husband and I have really grown. We've discovered so much about our faith and the church by being their sponsors and going through it all with them.'

Fixing meetings: How? When? Where?

The process can start just as soon as one person comes to ask to join the church, to find out more about Christianity, or whatever their approach may be. It begins with welcome and some kind of sponsoring by lay people of the newcomer. However, you may need to wait until there are more than one or two enquirers before linking them with church members to make up a group.

You may well have several groups running at the same time. Availability of rooms, number of enquirers, number of leaders and the time of year that people come forward all have a bearing. Some parishes have an enquirers group which runs most of the time to welcome people in the very earliest stage of their journeys and to feed them into learning and growing groups when they are ready for that.

You are faced with practical choices when setting up groups. The place where the group meets has an effect on how it develops. Our preference is for meetings in a home, but it may be right in some cases to use a room in the church or the church hall. Ordinary human comfort is important. It is an essential part of welcome. Hospitality is a sign of the church's love for people. So warmth, chairs that don't leave people with a stiff back for days afterwards, and easy lighting are all essential considerations in setting up a group meeting.

If the meeting is in someone's house, you have to decide whether it is a good or a bad thing for it to be the leader's home. It is usually easier not to have the double job of hosting and being responsible for the work of the meeting. Over the months it may be a good thing to move round different homes, so spreading the load.

When and how long should the session be? The answer depends

on the candidates. What is the best time for them? How are they affected by shift work or by family responsibilities? For some the best time may be evenings. Others prefer afternoons before their children come home from school. Others are coffee-morning people. Where there are families with children you need to consider whether the church ought to provide baby-sitters to relieve the candidates of having to pay for them.

Set a sensible time limit for the sessions and do your best to stick to it. Let it be agreed by all the members, so that anyone can feel free to leave when that time is up. An hour and a half or two hours is probably enough: any longer can be very tiring.

Make a decision about refreshments. Starting with tea or coffee helps break the ice and gives space for some people to arrive a bit later than others. Ending with refreshments at a definite time arranged beforehand makes a good stopping point when there is a danger of running on and on. A half-way break is the most difficult. It is hard to get the time right, and refreshments often disturb the flow of a meeting. Here is one vital word of warning. Beware of 'cake competitions'! If you are moving round different homes, try to establish an agreed level of hospitality and stick to it.

You will also need to decide how often the group will meet. There are several patterns to choose from. It could be regularly every week or every fortnight through the year. This could be too great a commitment for some people. Some groups meet in bursts of weekly meetings over six, eight or ten weeks and then have a break.

Some meet on Sundays after the service. There are also those, particularly in the USA, who follow the way of the early Church and meet with candidates during the second part of the parish Eucharist; they withdraw to 'break the Word' while the communicants break the bread.

People in the group also need to decide whether to stick to a set time and day of the week. There may be conflicting needs among the members which will mean you have to keep making adjustments. Life goes on and it is our experience that the introduction, as appropriate, of stories – the birth of a baby, an illness, examination passes or failures – fits in very well to this kind of working.

Leading a group

The first and most important thing for anyone invited to lead one of these groups to get clearly into their head is that they are not being asked to be a professor, schoolteacher or instructor. Their main job is to make it possible for other people to learn and grow as Christians. They are to be what today's jargon terms 'enablers'. Certainly, they are often going to be in a position to share some of their own experience of discipleship or to explain how they understand the Church's teaching. But they do not need to know it all. They don't have to have a degree in theology.

It may be a help to some leaders to have done a certain amount of Christian study, perhaps to have taken a Bishop's Certificate course, Education for Ministry, or some other sort of lay training. But it will be far more valuable to have done some training in the skills of group leadership, or to have had some experience in leading Lent groups, Bible studies or other forms of adult learning in small groups.

There are skills to be learnt, but they are very hard to pick up from a book. So what is written here is not in any sense a complete training to equip someone to be a group leader. Rather, it simply hints at the areas that need to be looked at, reviewed and developed in order for what happens in the life of a group to help the members to learn and grow in Christian discipleship.

It is a bit like being a good host or hostess at a party. The similarities are in the welcome, in making people feel at home, and treating them like valued guests. A good group leader sees that people are comfortable, helps them to relax and get on together, and tries to give everyone their chance to be heard when they want to say something.

On the other hand, the good group leader is not there to get the party going with a swing. A group meeting should not be all activity and noise: there needs to be time for reflection. Silence is not a failure – it often marks a high point in a session. Nor is conflict necessarily wrong. Imagine a roomful of eight or so people. That means not only eight different characters; it also means eight different experiences of life, eight different ways of meeting and thinking about God, and eight different ways of praying. In a group of eight people there are also 28 possible personal relationships. The conflict that may arise from these is real and needs to be faced honestly.

You will not be surprised if we say that one rapid round of introductions at the beginning of the first meeting is not sufficient. Several weeks will be needed in a gradual process of sharing. Time will be needed for the gradual unfolding of each member's story. At the most courteous level it is important to know a little about the everyday circumstances of each member of the group. Is Mary coming straight from work after a hurried sandwich on the bus? Does Frank have teenage children he is bringing up alone? Brenda can only just fit in cooking the evening meal and cleaning up after young children before she rushes out. Bridget's husband always comes to collect her and is waiting outside in the car at exactly 9 p.m. A little knowledge of these things is important as deeper discussion begins. They help everyone to know the frame of mind of their new friends and often go some way to explain the origins of the opinions they begin to express.

So, a very large part of the work of leading a group is about the relationships among the people who make up the group. It is about an atmosphere of respect, welcome and tact. It is not going too far to say that what good leadership requires is Christian love. It also needs some ability to manage people. This does not mean dominating them, ordering them about, or forcing them to do what you want. It means making it possible for the group to function well and to achieve what it is there for. We looked at some of the practicalities of this earlier on. There are also the personal skills to be learnt and practised, like ways of encouraging shy people to feel brave enough to contribute, and ways of encouraging the people who cannot stop talking and being the centre of attention to give way and let other people have a chance.

Preparation

If the group is to function well and achieve what it is there for, the leader's job is to *help* this to happen; not to *make* it happen, because everyone in the group shares the responsibility for that. Good leaders use their particular skills and gifts to enable everyone to learn and grow as disciples of Jesus. They act as coaches or guides to their companions as they travel together along the journey of faith and continuing conversion to Christ.

To do this well needs preparation and planning beforehand. Leaders who work in pairs can prepare and review sessions together, as well as give each other support during the session itself.

Catherine Widdicombe in *Meetings That Work: A Practical Guide to Teamworking in Groups* (2000) has this helpful diagram:

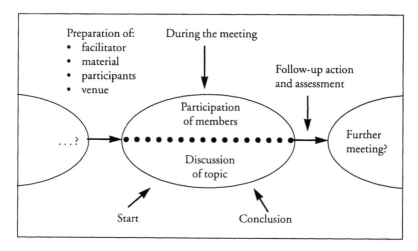

We want now to look rather more closely at that side of the work, though you will find more about the actual content of the process of learning and growing in the next chapter. Most leaders need the security of having some kind of structure to a group session in their minds before they start. There are the basics: you need to have a timetable to show when people should arrive; when you will have refreshments, if you think that is appropriate; when the working part of the session should start and finish; and when you expect people to leave. These are all things that ought to be agreed by everyone, but the leader has to take the initiative and offer suggestions.

You need to have a clear idea of the subject-matter for the session, and how you want to begin and develop the work. It is a great help if different members of the group offer to introduce topics in different sessions. It will soon become clear if there is particular interest or expertise in the group. The most reticent person may well flourish if they are allowed, or even encouraged, to bring some materials, pictures, music or verse which interests them. You need to know what kind of prayer you expect to be part of the session. You need to arrange any equipment you need, like Bibles or a flip-chart, a video- or a tape-recorder.

As well as needing the security of good planning, you also need to be flexible and move with the people in the meeting. After all, they are the reason for the session in the first place. Some groups have found it helpful to leave a 'blank' week in their topic planning. This gives a space for 'catching up' or to put in discussion of something important which has arisen in the course of discussion and needs development on a separate occasion. Sometimes the planned discussion itself has to be put on hold.

On one occasion a leader had planned a lovely evening on the Creation. She had worked out Bible readings. She had a video of volcanoes and Pacific islands. She brought a special music tape as a background to a period of quiet prayer. And it all went for nothing. The daughter of a middle-aged couple in the group had presented them with their first grandchild during the week and they could think of nothing else. All evening they and everyone else talked excitedly about babies. Quite spoiled the plan, but about Creation?

One useful planning guide for the basic structure of a session has these elementary pieces of preparation. They might only be the preparation of a few sentences or 'open' questions to get discussion going and the inclusion of 'summaries' at direction-changing

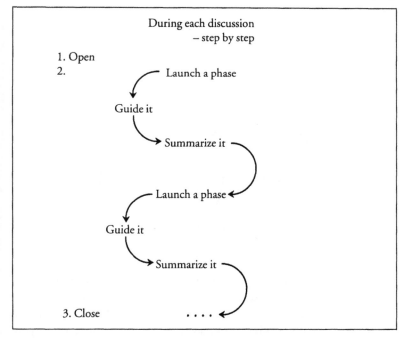

Launch, guide and summarize diagram

moments in an evening. Such a structure can prevent a discussion going round in too many circles. A good summary can clarify issues and prevent the 'bore' making the same point again when everyone else has moved on!

Leading a group is more like riding a horse with a will of its own than being in a train running along set tracks. Between these two extremes is a way of working with groups which might be helpful. It gives at least a framework within which most of the group members will feel more secure.

Some basic guides

'Content', the subject matter of the group sessions, and 'Process', the way the group works, both need care. People learn and grow through relating and absorbing the community life and the personal relationships within the group just as much as they do through discussing the material that forms the subject of the session programme.

The leader has to hold three important aspects of the work in balance – often in tension!

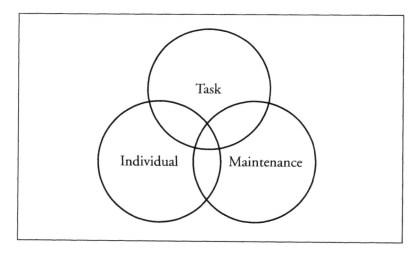

1. The *task* is the reason why people have met. The overall task of these groups is, of course, to accompany people into faith and to help them prepare for Christian initiation. When you meet, there is usually a subject you are working on or an activity you want to see achieved.

2. The group is made up of *individuals*, each of whom has their own needs and their own gifts to bring to the meeting. The leader's job is to see that as far as possible every member is given the opportunity to say what they have to say, that they are respected and helped to feel completely a part of what is going on. Under this heading comes the proper pastoral care that the leader has for the people in the group, a care that is shared with the others who also belong.

3. The life of the group itself needs *maintenance*. There are the practical provisions that need always to be kept in mind and there are the different aspects of management to watch. The leader needs to be alert to those factors that help or hinder the working of the group. Be aware of the relationships and pressures between people, as well as practical things like the arrangement of chairs and the courtesies of fixing suitable dates and times, and of letting people who are absent know the arrangements for next time.

If the early sessions have gone well but the leaders are worried about the 'balance' of the discussion, it is sometimes helpful for one of them to doodle a 'spider's web' of how the discussion is going. This sometimes makes it easier to spot who is not joining in very often – or at all. The dominant contributors will be even more obvious!

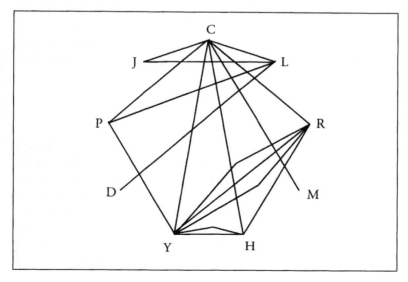

Success and failure

Most people like to be appreciated. They like to be told when they have done things well. It is important when you begin to do something that you know how to recognize whether or not it has been successful. There are not many exact markers of success and failure in leading this kind of group. You may have a good feeling at the end of a session because everyone seemed cheerful and chatty. You got through most of the material you had prepared on the resurrection of Jesus, so you feel it went well. It could be a couple of days before you realize that one of the group was intensely sad and worried, but could not bring herself to open up because of the overwhelming hearty feeling of the evening. She felt quite excluded but played along with the others because she was afraid she might break down and cry.

There are so many levels at which the life and work of a group go on. People's feelings, their understanding and the relationships between them are all involved. Much of the skill of leading is in being sensitive to as many of these different things as possible. You need to see how your group can travel together, accompanying one another into deeper awareness of faith in God, closer following of Jesus, and growing commitment to the work of the Kingdom in the world of everyday work, neighbourhood and home.

Success may not necessarily mean that all the scalps in your group will be offered to the bishop for baptism or confirmation. Success may well include someone deciding that the claims of the Gospel are too much for them to accept at this time. They may recognize that they are not yet ready. Your success is in being true to the truth that has been given to you and sharing it with them.

The absent host

Should the vicar or curate be there? Ideally, 'Faith on the Way' groups are led by lay people. The parish staff members will be the original convenors and will have played a large part in deciding who will be in which group. The temptation for an ordained person to be present in the groups should be resisted at all costs. It is much better for lay people to share faith in a mutually exploratory way. If there are leaders who introduce the subject every time the group meets, all they are doing is reinforcing the stereotype of the vicar as the fount of all wisdom. If the vicar is present, there is a surprising tendency for everyone to look to him or her for answers.

Exclusion is difficult for ministers. They love to be in on what might perhaps be one of the most interesting discussion groups of the week. It is important that someone from the group keeps the clergy briefed about progress and any potential or actual difficulties. Sometimes a special speaker might be invited; just occasionally such a person might be the vicar or the curate.

Reviewing the experience

Many of the best discussions will seem almost spontaneous. Frequently such ease will be an illusion. It will actually mean that the two leaders have done such a good piece of preparation that the flow will have seemed natural and almost spontaneous. The life of a good discussion begins well before the meeting and continues with reflection after it. Those present should never feel that they are being manipulated or that an inflexible structure is hemming them in. They may well just feel at ease because the leaders are at ease. This can come through good preparation of the basic structure of an evening, not through rigid planning of the content of a discussion.

Guiding and steering group discussion is a skill which comes through experience. Everyone who has ever led a group has made mistakes. Some of those mistakes we know about. Others, mercifully, will be kept from us for ever. Good group learning and good group leadership learning comes through reflection on the experience. Sometimes it is useful to take the last five or ten minutes of a discussion to review how it went and to plan for the next time. It is always useful for the leaders to take ten minutes after the group members have gone just to review the session. In that way the immediacy of the event is still very present and plans and corrections can be made.

After such a review there might also be time for a brief prayer for further help, for forgiveness and even of thanksgiving!

A simple warm-up exercise

Where I would like to be if I were not here	What I would really like to be called
My favourite meal	The person I most admire is . . .

References

Common Worship: Initiation Services (Church House Publishing, 1998)

Widdicombe, Catherine, *Meetings That Work: A Practical Guide to Teamworking in Groups* (The Lutterworth Press, 2000).

SIX

⁂

FAITH SHARING ON THE WAY

THIS CHAPTER IS PARTICULARLY IMPORTANT for those
people who are to lead groups. It will also be helpful for those
who act as companions to enquirers. At the end, there is a series of
worksheets drawing on material in the chapter and providing a short
course of training for group leaders.

In *Common Worship: Initiation Services* there is a commentary by
the Liturgical Commission which brings together what happens in
the liturgies and what happens in the preparation process.

> In preparing these services and additional supporting rites the
> Liturgical Commission had before it the following biblical
> framework, believing that baptism involves:
> * *separation* from this world – that is, the world alienated
>   from God, and
> * *reception* into a universal community centred on God,
>   within which
> * his children can *grow* into the fullness of the pattern of
>   Christ, and
> * a community whose *mission* is to serve God's Spirit in
>   redeeming the world.
> The liturgy of baptism needs to recognise that coming to faith
> in Christ involves a personal and social process (what the
> Toronto Statement calls the 'catechumenal process'). This is
> spelt out in *On the Way*: pre-baptismal preparation both for
> candidates and their families and for the community into
> which they will be baptised; continuing post-baptismal forma-
> tion, opening hearts and minds to the pattern centred on
> Christ crucified, a reversal of this world's ideas and values; and
> rites to mark stages on the way, so that they may be appropri-
> ated within the community. (Church House Publishing, 1998)

Faith sharing

The key to this chapter lies in the idea of sharing faith. What we are dealing with here is not instruction in the faith: it is about helping people to nurture a faith in God and Jesus, which is something more often caught than taught. The heart of it is the relationship between a man or a woman and the God revealed in the life, death and resurrection of Jesus Christ. It is celebrated in worship within his community, the Church, and lived out in the relationships, attitudes and choices of everyday life in the world.

Dialogue and conversation are at the heart of the process. The way people get to know one another and get to know about things is by talking and listening. For this to work well there needs to be genuine respect between the parties in the conversation. That is why in the work of the groups the keynotes of welcome, respect and trust are essential.

Story

Just as in some church circles 'sharing' is a word that has taken on a particular colour of its own, so 'story' has become a bit of a buzz word. Nevertheless, we are going to use both quite unashamedly.

As the introduction to *Common Worship: Initiation Services* puts it:

> In the spiritual formation of a new Christian there needs to be a healthy interaction between three aspects of the Christian life: *journey*, *story* and *pattern*. *Journey* is a major image in the narrative of scripture, from the call of Abraham through to the itinerant ministry of Jesus and beyond. As an image of human life and of the passage to faith it allows both for the integration of faith and human experience and also for the necessity of change and development.
>
> Closely related to journey is the importance in human and Christian experience of *story*. It is significant that the story of Paul's conversion is told three times in the book of Acts: Christian formation must allow an individual's story to be heard and to find its place within the unfolding story of faith as it appears in the Church and in the scriptures.
>
> Complementary to the ideas of journey or story is the theme

of *pattern* or *way*. Essential to Christian formation is the appro-
priation of pattern of belief, prayer and behaviour that give
structure and coherence to the Christian life. This is part of
what the earliest Christians recognised when they called themselves The Way. The report *On the Way* gave careful attention to
how patterns of life and faith are established in the life of the
Christian and the Church. These services seek to recognise that
journey and pattern are integral to the Christian life and need
to be reflected in any approach to Christian initiation. (Church
House Publishing, 1998)

Ask someone to tell you about themselves and it is more likely than
not that their reply will be to share a story that describes some aspect
of their life. 'I'm married and we've got three lovely children at
school.' 'I had a job as a fitter at Smith and Brown's, but I got laid off
last June and haven't been able to get another job since.' 'I used to be
a happy sort of person. Then my brother was killed on his motorbike
and I just don't seem to be able to get over it.'

Begin at the beginning

That is where the accompanied journey into faith begins. The only
place from which people can start is where they are. Far too often the
Church expects them to start from where the Church expects them
to be. Begin with listening. Of course enquirers have questions they
want to raise, and some of these, usually the most practical ones,
need to be answered early on. Deep spiritual questions about the
meaning of life and what it is all for take far longer; they need to be
answered not by a simple sentence from a teacher, but by reflection
on one's own personal experience and insight, together with reflection on God's revelation of himself in Jesus Christ and by entering
into the record of that revelation in scripture.

In the early part of the journey the work of the group is centred on
getting to know one another. People are invited to tell their own
stories. This can mean either telling some of the story of my life (the
bits I feel comfortable about sharing) or talking about what really
matters to me. Different people at different times in their lives will
want to do one or the other. In either case, people are sharing what is
important to them. It matters to Winston that his mother came from

Barbados. It matters to Jenny that her little girl has to go into hospital next week for an operation. It matters to Brian and Kylie that the doctor has given his father only a few more months to live. Bob and Ellen just live to see Liverpool at the top of the Premier League.

To listen to people's stories and encourage them to tell them does not mean being inquisitive. You need to be sensitive and not tread heavily where you have not been invited. It is more than a way of simply getting to know people better; it is starting with people where they feel themselves to be. Even more than that, it is trying to make it possible to discern where God is in their lives and where they are able to be open to him. The place where we are often most open to God is where we are most concerned about something or someone. It is where our feelings and our interest are most alive; where we hurt or where we want most deeply.

The Gospel story

Conversations involve more than one person. The dialogue here is between the stories of individuals and the story of the Christian Gospel. People with their histories, their interests and concerns come face to face with the Good News of God's love shown in Jesus. There is opportunity and space for both the person and the Gospel to interact, to challenge and to respond, as someone brings their deep concerns to the God they meet in his story or as that story enters into their heart.

'When you told us that story about Jesus healing the man who was lying paralysed by the pool, it made me think about myself. I wonder whether I'm just sitting back and waiting for other people to do things for me when I could probably get up and get going myself.'

'That elder brother who was cross when the other one was given a party. It's like that in my family. We've sort of cut Joan off since she got into trouble with the police over drugs. We ought really to make it up with her, I suppose.'

When we say 'Gospel story', we admit we are using shorthand. We mean something that, of course, includes the New Testament gospels, but also reflects the whole inheritance of the Church to which we belong. We are talking about the Good News which today's Christian has to share with today's enquirer who lives in today's world.

The Good News is there in the events we read about in the Bible. It is the story of God's self-giving love for his people, the story of his covenant relationship with the people of the Old Testament, Israel, and following them with the New Testament Church and those who have belonged to the community of the Body of Christ over the succeeding centuries. The Bible contains one over-arching story of God's initiative and people's response. It is also made up of countless different stories. When we use it as a base for the learning and introduction of newcomers to the faith, people can hear and react both to the overall story and to the different stories within it.

This reflects the method Jesus used when he taught in parables. A parable is a good story in its own right. What makes it a tool for teaching is the way in which it sparks off some kind of response in the hearer. Maybe it challenges you to review your own behaviour.

Think, for example, of the parable of the rich man and Lazarus; notice its sharp contrast between the lifestyles of the man feasting indoors and the sore-infested beggar outside. Maybe it opens your spiritual vision to respond in some way to God.

If the anxious housewife can get so excited at finding the coin she lost, what a wonderful thought that God can get excited when he finds someone like me turning towards him!

What is happening here is more than the kind of work that is sometimes done in Bible study groups, which are often based quite heavily 'in the head'. In this kind of group, as people try together to deepen their understanding of the message, analysis, meaning and cross-references take up a lot of their time. In the story-to-story dialogue we are suggesting here, the meaning of a passage is naturally an important part of the work, but it is not the main part or the most effective.

The question is not so much 'What does this passage mean, how do I explain it, or how does it relate to this or that aspect of Christian belief?' Rather, it is: 'As I hear this passage, what does it mean to me? What does this passage tell me about Jesus, about God? How do I hear it? Where does it key into my life, my experience and my attitudes?' This leads on to the converting question: 'So what changes does this passage ask of me?'

There is any number of different ways a group can open out the Bible for its members. Here is one example which are designed to help people bring the scripture story face to face with their own lives.

An African model

In this way there is no need for people to read the text. It is a matter of listening and reflecting:

- Opening prayer to gather the members together and focus the session.
- Ask people to listen for a word or phrase that stands out or speaks for them. Read the gospel passage aloud slowly and deliberately.
- One minute of silence.
- Invite everyone simply to say the word or phrase that touched them. Do not discuss!
- Read the gospel passage again.
- Tell the group you will give them five minutes of silence to be with the gospel (or three minutes if they are new to it). Be quiet for that time.
- Invite them to note what they hear in their heart, what the passage touches in their life. They could write it down.
- Divide into groups of not more than four or five, perhaps twos and threes, to speak of what they have got from the gospel passage. It is very important that they use the word 'I' and own their personal experience and insight, rather than say what others believe. It is not a time for discussing or preaching or solving the problems of other people.
- Read the gospel passage again.
- Ask people to consider what, in the light of the meeting so far, they believe God wants from them this week. How is God inviting them to change? What are they taking home with them this week? Specific answers are important, rather than responses like 'God wants me to be good for ever and ever!'
- Again, in small groups, share these answers.
- Gather the group together for a closing prayer with perhaps one of the Sunday readings, open prayer, silence and singing.
- Give details of the next meeting and the passages to be read.

The Church

The Good News is not to be found only in the pages of the Bible. It can be recognized in the changed lives of the people of God over the centuries. Anyone coming to Christian faith in the present century is aware in one way or another that they are entering into a long inheritance of spiritual tradition. For some it may be the tradition that is expressed in the local parish church built in 1857 or in the fifteenth century. It surfaces in the worship that takes place in that church with roots that stretch back to the Last Supper, to the Divine Office of early Benedictine monasteries, or the hymns of the Wesleys. It also causes confusion because it carries the echoes of controversies and hurts from many past ages. These still break out and distort God's loving welcome as church men and women voice partisan battle cries or narrow the vastness of his message into tight little doctrinal statements.

The word 'tradition' simply means something that is handed on. Companions and group leaders have a duty to pass on the tradition that they have received from others. That, after all, seems to be why the Bible exists. It was written, put together and handed on within the Church. Within the wide tradition of Christianity, the Bible has its uniquely privileged position as a record of what has happened in the past and as a guide to today's Christian living and believing.

In working with enquirers and new Christians there should be a conscious balance between the demands of what is inherited in statements and written documents and the immediate contemporary meeting between a person and Christ present in the telling of the Good News.

Syllabus or demand feeding?

We have suggested that, at least in the earlier part of the journey, much of the work in the groups is led by the stories that the enquirers have to tell. The material for discussion is what they bring rather than what the leaders think they ought to be teaching. We have also suggested that unless this listening to the stories of the people in the group continues to be recognized and valued as a strong element in the life of the group, it will not fulfil its purpose of accompanying men and women along the journey of conversion. God is at work in people's lives in real events, real relationships and real feelings, perceptions and reactions.

Group leaders sometimes say, 'Fine. I see it's important to give the enquirers their say, but how are we to know what to do in the sessions?'

From experience, we suggest that the answer goes something like this: 'Don't worry too much about doing it right. It's normal for parishes to start with fairly structured sessions in the groups. Then, as they get more confident over a couple of years, they become far more flexible.'

It is normal for a parish starting out to use the process to carry into it something from what has happened in the past. So at first, group leaders are likely to follow the kind of pattern that the minister used in his adult confirmation classes. They will ask for a syllabus of topics to be covered and suggestions for each session – a kind of lesson plan. This should be a co-operative effort with the minister and the leaders planning and reviewing the sessions as they go through the season. For some it may be right to start from one of the many published course outlines, but they should also work hard to move the focus of attention away from the subject-matter and the leader towards the enquirers in the group and towards the idea of dialogue between them and the subject.

Forget the attitude that sees the Christian education of adult lay men and women as the same kind of thing that the clergy did for a university degree or at theological college – but made simple for simple folk! It may be right to have as a basis for the course something that covers the main headings of Christian belief and the life and practice of the Church. There are several textbooks available for leaders who want to work along those lines.

We hope that in the actual meetings of the group, people will ease out beyond the boundaries that are set by the image of the teacher who is expert in the Christian tradition instructing the ignorant about the mysteries. It is for all group members to travel together into an experience of living faith and to put that faith into practice in the decisions and relationships of their daily life, as people who are themselves caught up in God's mission of peace and justice to his world.

There is a very fine syllabus already given to us in the Christian year. Many local churches work on the principle that they do not need any other textbook in the catechumenate apart from the readings which, Sunday by Sunday, tell the story of God's dealings with his people. Perhaps this 'lectionary-based catechesis' is specially valuable when the sessions take place on a Sunday at the time of the main service. Where this happens there should be an opportunity for co-ordination between the preacher and the work of the group so that some kind of integrated teaching can take place.

A half-way house between the syllabus approach and the more open way could be found in having a checklist of themes that should be covered during the course. Again we suggest that this is something to be developed jointly by clergy and lay people involved, so that together they can work out what could be called a local baptismal creed – the things that we in our church believe people should have covered, understand or be at home with before they come to be baptized or confirmed. Working out such a list is a useful exercise in itself!

Checklist

We expect most Christians would include in their checklist most of the headings that follow, although different communities will put different emphases on some parts. You may well have other important topics you want to add.

❏ *Prayer.* How can you help people into a relationship with God? What place does it have in personal life and the work of the group? (This is the subject of Chapter 7.)

❏ *Public worship.* How are people helped to take part in church? How does participation contribute to our Christian formation as individuals and as the Holy People of God? The shape of the Eucharist and other services. The books, the hymns and the language.

❏ *Creation.* What is the world we live in? What is it for? What does it mean to say God is the Creator? What is the responsibility of human beings in the world or for the world?

❏ *'The Fall'.* If we believe God is good and loves us, why is there such trouble and wrong in the world? What is the status of humanity: good, but distorted by sin? Or totally lost? What does 'sin' mean?

❏ *God and his people.* What do we mean by 'covenant', the 'Chosen People', as we read the Old and New Testaments?

❏ *Incarnation.* In Jesus, God took on human flesh. How do we express the faith that Jesus is both fully God and fully human?

❏ *The ministry of Jesus.* Proclaiming the Good News of the

Kingdom, healing and teaching. How are the parables and miracles Good News for us and for our time?

❑ *The Passion and death of Jesus, his resurrection.* What do these mean for us? How do we hear words like 'redemption', 'atonement', 'salvation' or 'sacrifice'?

❑ *Pentecost and the Holy Spirit.* What do they mean for us? Where do you stand in relation to Charismatic Renewal? Where do you see evidence of the Holy Spirit in your relationships?

❑ *'One, Holy, Catholic and Apostolic Church'.* What do these individual words mean to you? How are they expressed on the ground in your locality? What does the Church mean to you? How important is it in your day-to-day walk with God?

❑ *The Bible.* How are people to read it? What does 'This is the Word of the Lord' mean to you?

❑ *The Church's ministry.* What are bishops, priests and deacons? What is their responsibility? What is the responsibility of lay people in the Church?

❑ *Authority.* Where does authority lie in the Church? What is the authority of the ordained ministers, of the laity and of the whole people of God? How is it exercised and how should it be exercised?

❑ *Right and wrong.* What areas of moral choice are important for you? How do you choose?

❑ *The mission of the Church.* What is evangelism? How can you/do you bear witness to the Gospel in everyday life? How can/should the Church serve those in need?

❑ *Life in the church.* How does the parish work? What is a Parish Council for? How is church life funded and what is your responsibility in this?

❑ *Life in the world.* What difference does being a Christian make to life at home, at work or in the community? What is the relationship between Christianity and politics? What are the things about modern life that make it hard to be a Christian, and how can you deal with them?

The four texts

These checklist headings echo the elements of *journey, story* and *pattern* which we quoted at the beginning of this chapter. They draw out the elements of belief, of behaviour, of prayer, of change and belonging which are essential parts of the way to Christian faith. *Rites on the Way* follows the RCIA in offering liturgies which mark these essentials by presenting the enquirer with key texts which have been handed down over the Christian centuries as part of the tradition of the Church. They are Jesus' Summary of the Law; the Lord's Prayer; the Apostles' Creed; and the Beatitudes (see Chapter 9).

There is no particular point at which these liturgies take place. It could be during the final time leading to baptism or it could be at some appropriate earlier occasion when the subject matter of the text has been worked on by the group.

Local adaptation

It must by now be clear that we are trying to avoid writing a blueprint to be followed slavishly in every situation: quite the opposite. We believe that plants will only grow well if they are cared for properly and rooted in the soil that is right for them. So it would be wrong of us to lay down our own personal colour of belief and practice as a norm for all to follow. Rather, what we hope to do is to present some guidelines that you may use or not as you wish.

People who come to join your church have chosen to do so. There are alternatives they could have chosen but did not. This means that the process and the content of groups ought to be true to the ethos of your church.

Conversion and the whole person

Learning and growing in discipleship involves change; in other words, conversion. Companions and leaders represent the Church and are there to accompany people through their conversion to faith in Jesus Christ. We suspect that many will feel that they are quite inadequate for this task, largely because they have a particular picture in their mind of what conversion means. Thus it may be useful to think a bit more widely around what this learning, growing and changing might mean.

Human beings are creatures with a body, a mind, senses, instincts, emotions and a will. We can experience all these aspects of what it means to be a person. It is rather harder to experience what it means to have a soul. We have an idea of what 'spiritual' might mean; it often refers to what we have felt or come to understand in ways that go beyond any of the faculties we have just mentioned. There is a sense in which when we make important choices, our will draws on something deep within us which we can call our soul. It is more than personality or character, though 'who I really am' could well come near to describing what 'soul' might mean.

I am one person: I cannot be split up into different departments. Intelligence, feelings, will and all the other faculties work together as I live my life. But there is more to me than that. It is hard to imagine what it could be like to be a person totally and utterly alone. So much of who I am is linked with how I relate to people and to things outside of myself. We are individual men and women, certainly, but it is as we live out our lives in all sorts of different relationships that we grow into fuller people.

So much by way of background to our thinking about conversion to Christ. If a journey from little or no Christian faith towards belief, commitment and membership of the Church is to mean anything worthwhile, it simply has to involve the whole of a person, all those different aspects and faculties. A complete personality is engaged.

One or other side of a person will be more important than the others. For some people the opening to belief may come through events and choices that throw up questions of right and wrong. They may be challenged in their conscience about things they have done or said in the past; they realize that they need to be forgiven somehow. Or it may be that they are faced with terribly hard decisions in life which they sense they are quite inadequate to deal with on their own.

Questions about the meaning of life are the entry point for quite a few. How are we to reconcile human suffering and the unfairness of life with the goodness, truth and beauty that we also see around us? Can the vast, complex universe be explained as something that just happened in a random way, or is there a purpose behind it?

For some people, God seems to take a hand directly. Far more people than usually admit it have had some kind of spiritual experience, an awareness that comes to them of a reality beyond themselves.

Feelings and emotions often play an important part in this process of change, just as they do in many important choices and changes that people make in their lives. Fear or attraction, a longing for the warmth of love and acceptance, the excitement of belonging to something alive or perhaps even the enjoyment of music or a lovely building – any of these can be the starting point or an aid to the development of conversion.

A choice to be made

For most people conversion is a gradual process. There may well be high and low points along the way. Some of these may be dramatic changes or experiences charged with strong emotion. Some may involve costly decisions about lifestyles or behaviour. What we want to emphasize is that if the journey of learning and growing in faith and loyalty is to be true, it has to be concerned with the whole of personality. Feelings matter, the mind matters, our perceptions matter. In the end, what matters most are the choices we make.

One of the hardest things to describe in the process of conversion is who is responsible for it. In the list of the aspects of what it means to be a person there are some faculties where you are in charge and making the decisions. You can see or you can shut your eyes. You can respond to someone in a conversation or choose to keep quiet. You can try to come to a decision or just shelve it. But feelings and emotions tend to happen whether you want them to or not. Spiritual experiences are like that too; you cannot choose to have them. When it comes to choosing whether or not to believe, to make an act of faith or to commit your life to God, there is a sense in which you are both in charge of the decision and not in charge. You change the direction of your life; you alter your attitudes towards God and towards other people; you open your heart to a new kind of love for your Creator and Saviour. Or do you? Is it just as true to say that your heart is opened, your attitudes and your direction are changed for you?

The truth is that the initiative lies with God who works in us and with us, using many different sides of our personality. But we also have a responsibility of our own, to agree or to refuse, to say 'Yes' or to say 'No'.

And so . . .

Just as the whole of a person is involved in coming to conversion, so too we should expect that the effects of conversion will show in all aspects of personality and relationships. Here again, as all of us know from our own painful experience, we are talking about a gradual, often shamingly slow, process rather than a sudden and immediate flash of total perfection. Continuing conversion throughout life means a deepening in our awareness of God and in our relationship with him. It also means a continual recognition of our need for greater love, greater truth, fuller holiness, as we are being shaped into the person that God has designed us to become.

Worksheets
Training Group Leaders (several sessions).

Preparation
Remind yourself about the earlier chapters of this book, especially Chapter 5.

Introduction
This set of worksheets gives outline ideas for several sessions which will work best if they take place in a group of between five and ten people. It may be advisable to have leaders from different churches in the neighbourhood meeting together in order to get suitable numbers.

It may also be advisable to invite a trainer with some experience to lead the sessions. Diocesan lay ministry advisers, adult education departments or church societies should be able to help here.

Recognize that you will learn by your own experience of taking part in the meetings of this group. Notice your own feelings and reactions and be prepared to talk about them.

Practical points
1. Make diary dates for as many leader training sessions as are likely to be needed. Fix venues for these sessions.
2. Make diary dates through the next few months for review sessions with the leaders and the clergy together.

Training topics
Separate sessions may concentrate on different areas:

4A The practice of leading a group.
4B The relationship between Content and Process.
4C Ways of working with people's own stories.
4D Ways of working with the Bible and the tradition of the Church.

Worksheet 4A: Leading a Group

1. Reflect together on what has happened in the meetings that members of the group have been involved in so far.
   (a) What has been the experience of the members and of the leaders?
   (b) How well have you achieved your tasks?
   (c) How has each member been helped or hindered by life within the group and by the leadership of the group?
   (d) What problems have had to be faced and how have they been dealt with?
2. Make a list of topics for discussion. Let each member act as leader for one of the topics for fifteen minutes, first giving a short introduction. Spend five minutes reviewing how each session went.

Worksheet 4B: Content and Process

1. Spend time reflecting together on Chapters 5 and 6.
   (a) What help do leaders need in order to feel confident about faith sharing?
   (b) How do you feel about a syllabus or a checklist of topics for the group?
   (c) What effect has the training so far had upon the faith, confidence or understanding of members of the group?
   (d) What would be the important elements of a 'Baptism Creed' in your local church? What do you think should be the marks of readiness for membership?
2. List the important things that have come out of the session.
3. Pray together about these important things.

Worksheet 4C: Individual Stories

1. Spend time alone on your own story (perhaps in preparation at home for this session). You could use one of the suggestions in Worksheet 3B. Enter into something that is important to you (for whatever reason) and that you are prepared to talk about with someone else.
2. In pairs, spend half an hour on each other's stories. Give attention to the quality of your listening. Be aware not only of the human interest and importance of the story, but also of where you can discern God at work in the other person's life.
3. In the main group, share what has happened in the pairs.
4. Close with a simple, structured time of worship that expresses what has happened during the session.

Worksheet 4D: Bible and Tradition

The session is to be spent working from a Bible passage. The purpose is to let the Bible story have its effect on people's lives, rather than spend time analysing it in an intellectual way.

Preliminary work

Choose the passage to be used. This could be the next Sunday's gospel or a passage which seems to be particularly appropriate to the work of the group. Suggestions include the call of the disciples (Mark 1:15–20 or John 1:35–42); the healing of the paralysed man (Mark 2:1–12 or Luke 5:17–26); the stilling of the storm (Mark 4:35–41); Zacchaeus (Luke 19:1–10) or, from the story of the early Church, Philip and the Ethiopian (Acts 8:26–40).

Task

1. Use the 'African Method' in Chapter 6 or some other way to work with the chosen passage. (If the group is large enough, divide into two so that each group can use different methods.) Spend about three-quarters of an hour on this.
2. Break for refreshments.
3. Spend twenty minutes in a review of the work with the Bible. (If the group divided, this will include each group sharing their experience with the other.)
4. Close with a simple, structured time of worship which expresses what has happened during the session.

Worksheet 4E: Enquiry and Welcome

To help group leaders and clergy in the planning of the early meetings of the groups.

Practical points

1. Decide on the people who will be in the group(s). This may depend on a previous decision about whether or not you need an 'Open Space' occasion to meet enquirers before the actual process begins.
2. Decide what meetings are needed before the Service of Welcome. This will depend on how well you know the enquirers and how committed you sense they are to joining the programme.
3. If not already done, fix the date of the Service of Welcome.

Session planning

Consider the 'style' of meetings in the early part of 'the Way'. What have been your experiences so far in these preparation sessions? Look at the areas of welcome, story-telling, listening and faith sharing. What has been good and needs to be incorporated in the group sessions, and what has not been helpful and should be avoided?

Design outlines for the first two meetings. Note what the purpose of the session is. Decide how you will open the session and what work you propose for the group. If you are working as a pair of leaders, decide who will do what in the session.

Decide how you will arrange the room, what refreshments you are to have, and who will provide them. See what equipment, like pencil and paper, books, video etc., you are likely to need. (It is better to have more than you actually use than to run out.)

Reference

Common Worship: Initiation Services (Church House Publishing, 1998).

SEVEN

PRAYING TOGETHER ON THE WAY

THIS CHAPTER IS WRITTEN for companions and group leaders as they help people to grow in their relationship with God in Jesus. There are skills and attitudes which can be acquired in order to feel confident in this area and to do it well. Some are covered here; others can be learned only from other people in dialogue and as relationships develop. In a growing number of areas there are courses in spiritual direction both for beginners and for people with some experience. These often include an element of support, review and continuing development for those who are engaged in this ministry.

Praying in the group

Praying together is part of the work of the group accompanying adults into faith. It can take many different forms: sometimes open, free prayer; sometimes following a simple liturgy. It is different from services in church and is more personal and intimate. It is also different from praying on your own.

Praying together should be more than simply a formal opening or closing with prayer. There should be a space for perhaps a Bible passage, some comment, some reflection and sharing of ideas, reactions and concerns from people in the group; a time of silence and a time for open prayer, spoken or silent, by the members. In the worksheets there are suggestions which may help the group to devise a simple liturgy as part of its work. Short acts of worship can grow out of the activities of the session. There may well be opportunity for using everyday objects or simple actions as symbols of prayer in the group.

Talking about prayer

People can be shy about matters of faith. They are reluctant to talk about spirituality. You may pray, and prayer may be an important part of your life, but you also may find it hard to be open. You feel it is private; perhaps you also feel it is inadequate, not good enough. This combination of not wanting to parade something that is intimate and not wanting to expose what is seen as a weakness means that, while many may be able to talk about their belief in God, they recoil from speaking about their friendship with Jesus. They also feel chary about opening the subject of how others pray. But a developing friendship with God is essential; it is at the very centre of all that we are about.

The community prays

Prayer is the work of the Church, the Body of Christ. As the Christian community we, ordinary men and women, are intimately caught up in the eternal relationship of love between Jesus and the Father in the Holy Spirit. That is the basis for our activity of praying. The worship that is part of the life of the church comes first; it is one of the givens. During his lifetime, the prayer of Jesus was the open offering of himself to the will of the Father. The church's offering continues this prayer and is caught up in the eternal relationship of Father and Son in the Holy Spirit. Each Christian has their place and their part in it.

This belief about prayer is expressed in what goes on in the local church on a Sunday or on weekdays and in the wonderfully varied ways in which men and women give their attention to God privately on their own and publicly with others.

Public prayer

There are several ways of sorting and labelling prayer. One is into 'public' and 'private'. Public prayer is the worship that the Christian community does together. The way it worships depends on the tradition of the local church as it meets to offer praise, thanks, penitence and prayer. Most follow some sort of pattern, often a formal liturgy as in the Eucharist.

For some newcomers and enquirers, as for some established church members, this joining in public worship may be their main, even their only, way of praying. In a week that is full of busy-ness, activity, pressure or strain, the church service stands as an oasis of refreshment when they can concentrate on their relationship with God.

Public prayer is the prayer of the community. It has an ongoing quality about it, its own life and validity. I take part in it, I also have my part in it. As a Christian, it is where I belong. It may also be the occasion when I say my own prayers, bring my own needs to God and offer my own gratitude. But the most important thing about public liturgy is that it is corporate; it expresses the truth that Christians belong together in the Body of Christ.

Private prayer

Praying on your own or with one or two other people is different from public worship. Most of the rest of this chapter is about the ways people pray as individuals and how they vary. The diagram on page 102 is designed as a help in looking at the different parts of ourselves that we bring into our praying. It is not complete, it does not answer every situation, but we offer it as a starting-point.

Words and systems

Some people have words as the main vehicle of their praying. The idea of saying prayers comes naturally to them, either praying aloud or simply forming words and phrases in their mind. They like books of prayers written by other people or collections that they have made for themselves. Sometimes they write their own prayers.

Such people like order and system in their relations with God. Daily prayers follow a pattern in which they feel at home; it is what they always do. Lists are helpful: lists of people, causes and institutions to pray for.

'Chatting with my friend God', is how one person described her prayer, going through the day and referring to him things that have happened, decisions that have to be made, problems and worries encountered. For her and for many others, prayer is a conversation either spoken or formed in the heart with a God who cares and listens and who occasionally is sensed to be replying.

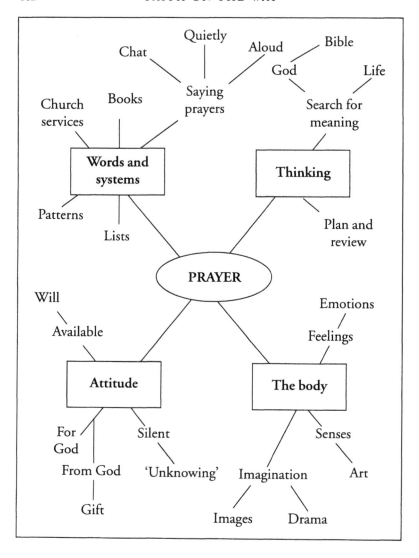

Thoughts

Thinking about God, using your conscious mind to get in touch with him, to try to understand who he is or what he is about, is the natural way to pray for some people. The search for a meaning in life is about how to explain things, how to make sense of it all. If you use Bible study notes, for instance, you will be at home with the sort that end with 'questions for discussion'. You may well like to use a Bible that has references giving other passages to compare.

Faced with a problem, someone who prays in this way will spend time working it through with God. Their prayers often give space for planning, looking ahead to the day's events in their morning prayers, and to review at the end of the day.

Brian had been seriously ill: he nearly died. He told me afterwards that he had not been able to pray. He knew how ill he was. He recognized that he was facing the prospect of eternity and he found that he spent a lot of time in his illness trying to think what it would mean and where God came into it. He tried to face up to some part of his own death. Normally he prayed quite differently with a mixture of set prayers and a feeling of warmth towards God. He found it hard to recognize that during his illness it was a case not of not being able to pray, but of learning to pray in a quite different way.

There are all the 'Why?' questions that spring from the tragedies and meaningless disasters of personal and international life. How are people to come to terms with a loving God in the face of famines and injustice?

The body

This next section is about a very important part of being a whole person. It is to do with how we perceive, how we feel, and how we create. It looks at how that aspect of being human which is not to do with words and thinking leads into or expresses the spiritual dimension of our lives. Parts of this concern our bodies, our senses and our emotions. It is also about our imagination and fantasies. We are talking about perceptions and faculties which are, to use rather technical words, 'affective' rather than 'intellectual' – praying in pictures, entering into stories, living out dramas, carried away by music, expressing your relationship with God in song or in dance.

Prayer is concerned with the physical in many different ways. Yoga has taught Western men and women the importance of posture, exercise and breathing in a search for well-being and a balanced life. They are important aspects of Christian prayer too. Notice how your body is when you pray. Are you relaxed or tense, floppy or alert? Does it help to stand or kneel, to sit or to lie down? What does it mean for you to open your hands, palms upwards, and gently lift them to waist level . . . to shoulder level . . . to high above your head? What differences do you recognize when you are kneeling or sitting, standing or lying down as you pray? Movement and dance can also have their place in prayer, even when you are alone.

Feelings and images

For people who use the Bible to pray in an imaginative way, the gospels are not a quarry for texts to relate to other texts or for evidence to support this or that belief. They contain stories to be entered into. They present people to be met and a Jesus who met people in particular ways. He offers acceptance, forgiveness and reconciliation. The prayer of images and imagination opens an important side of a person to God. Rather than thinking about incidents in life or in the gospels, the person praying in this way enters into them in their imagination to experience the meaning for themselves.

Over thousands of years prayer has been sung or played on a musical instrument. If you appreciate Handel's *Messiah*, it is almost impossible to read the Bible texts on which it is based without hearing echoes of the music. You may find that when in your prayers you want to express praise to God, it is often the tune of a well-known hymn of worship that means more than its words.

It can be the same for sight as it is for hearing. Things you see can move you to prayer, whether they are natural sights or works of art. It could be a sunset over the loch between the mountains, the soaring vaults of a great cathedral, or the colours and depth of an oil painting. It may help your prayer to have a lighted candle, or perhaps you find it easier to pray with your eyes gently closed.

Then there is your imagination. It is about images, of course, but to use imagination in prayer is more than simply creating images. It is letting the non-rational, non-intellectual side of your personality have its proper place in your journey into God. People spend time happily fantasizing about all sorts of things: success at work, sexual encounters, what to do if they win the Lottery. There is also the darker side of fantasy: the fears and anxieties that come to scare and disturb you, awake as well as dreaming. Fear of death or injury to someone you love in an accident. Even the simple fear that you didn't turn off the oven when you left home for holiday.

This prayer of images and imagination opens another side of a person to God. Rather than thinking about incidents in life or in the gospels, praying in this way helps you to enter into them in your imagination and to experience their meaning for yourself.

Emotions play a large part in human life and they have their proper place in praying. For some people, feelings are the heart of their prayer; for others just one aspect of it. But it is always worthwhile to notice how you feel, how you react. Feeling is more immediate than thinking. It often indicates what is deepest, perhaps where God is at work in the depths of your life. Notice feelings of warmth or distance, of love or shame or fear; being moved to prayer by anxiety about someone you love or by being afraid for yourself; enjoying a sense of comfort, reassurance and being in tune with God. In these and many other ways the affective side of our nature is either a way into prayer, a way of praying, or a way of experiencing the effect of prayer.

Attitudes

Feelings can often be a bridge leading into this fourth kind of prayer. Warmth, excitement, fear, anticipation, desire – all these, focused on God, can be a way towards the 'Prayer of Attitudes'. In this you quietly direct your whole self towards God in love and openness. It may have an emotional content; you may have arrived by way of conversation with God, by way of thinking, or by way of imagination or feelings, but in this way of prayer you simply make yourself available to contemplate God as he is, and give him your attention, open to be aware of him, waiting in his presence.

It is a way of prayer that, because of its nature, is very hard to describe in words. Even pictures are little help. The title of a medieval book about it, *The Cloud of Unknowing*, emphasizes that this is not a prayer of the intellect. There is not much activity. You pray more by waiting, by being available. My image is of a she-cat hunting. She does not prowl dramatically about, looking eager and menacing. She sits, at once alert and relaxed, and she listens. Her hunting consists largely of being aware of every sound in the long grass and discerning the distinct rustle made by a mouse or a vole.

When people talk about their experience of this 'contemplative' prayer, they make very tentative statements; they often use double negatives like 'I don't really know how to describe what happened in my prayer time today, but I know God was not absent.' You are involved in a prayer that takes place at a different level from thoughts and feelings. It is deeper and belongs to the most important part of your nature: your will. The choices you make and what you decide show what you really believe to be most important and valuable in your life. Reginald Somerset Ward, a notable Anglican spiritual director in the first half of this century, used to say 'The will is the voice of the soul.'

This way of praying more than any other illustrates the true purpose of prayer. It is for God. It points away from self, from my thoughts, feelings or concerns, and dwells entirely on God as God is – both the source of the prayer and its aim.

Spiritual companionship

Probably anyone reading these brief classifications will recognize something of their own experience in several – perhaps all – of them. You may settle on one or two that are closest to your present way of praying. All are perfectly good and valid ways of praying for any Christian. You may want to explore those which, up to now, have not been for you. There may be others in your group who will share their different experiences and who will now be able to accompany you.

A Christian accompanying an enquirer should recognize how their friendship with God is growing and help it to develop in a way that is right for them. Our spiritual lives vary and an enquirer's way may be quite different from their companion's. What suits one person can be quite improper for another.

Beware of expecting another person to switch to your way of praying. Accept the truth that God has made people different and that he has given to each of us our own way to draw nearer. Be prepared to listen for the ring of truth in other people's experience, however strange it may seem to you.

This work of accompanying demands an ability to listen, a gift of discernment, and a certain degree of background knowledge. It requires enough confidence and enough humility. This confidence comes from having accepted that it is a proper part of the accompanying ministry to be a coach in spiritual matters and from having sufficient understanding of the basic principles of spirituality. It is also important to have backing and help from somebody else who is acting as your own spiritual guide.

This humility comes from recognizing that the person you are accompanying has their own true spirituality and that your work is only to help them, under God's guiding, to grow into the kind of people it is possible for them to become.

John Westerhoff writes:

The best guide on a spiritual journey is one who does not need to be helpful or needed, one who does not try to bear the responsibility of another life, but who can leave others in the hands of God – and get a good night's sleep. It is to take responsibility for one's own spiritual growth and to be with others as they do likewise. (Westerhoff, 1983)

The givenness of prayer

Prayer is a dialogue; it is something that is a gift from God. This makes it possible for someone to pray. This is the inspiration. Without God there would be nothing. On the other hand, prayer is a human work. It requires effort on our part; it requires that we choose to put aside some time for it. We have to make ourselves available. We have continually to be recalling our wandering attention from all sorts of other thoughts, daydreams and interests to the business of seeking God.

The most common danger at all stages along the road to prayer seems to be the danger of over-worrying and guilt at the thought of being a failure. Prayer is a gift, and our part in it is response to a gift.

In the four-way analysis of prayer on page 102 there can be seen to be a gap. The Charismatic Renewal in churches of all denominations speaks strongly of prayer as a gift from God, prayer as meeting a God who is Spirit, in human response to his call. This emphasis on the grace, the gift or, in religious technical language, the charism of praying should be recognized as a firm counter-balance to the common feeling that we need to work harder and harder to succeed in spirituality.

Variations and change

People who have prayed over a length of time, several months perhaps, several years certainly, will know that the 'temperature' of their praying varies considerably. There are times when it feels warm and meaningful to pray; God is real and near. It is quite easy. However, there are other times when all that disappears. Praying is a cold, dull and lonely activity. It becomes difficult to persuade yourself that there is anything in it. God seems totally absent, if he exists at all. Such variations are common to all praying Christians. 'I used to be able to pray. I used to enjoy it. But now I can't. It doesn't work for me anymore.'

To put it simply, probably far too simply, there are two possible reasons for this experience of the emptiness of prayer. There is also another often given, but very often mistaken. This usually false reason is the one that the person is most likely to offer themselves. It is that they are not trying hard enough; they think they ought to pray 'better', whatever that means, and they give themselves a bad time over it. This is a perfectly natural reaction, but in my experience it is usually wrong. It is an example of the danger of seeing prayer as a human activity only. It forgets the 'givenness'.

What is far more likely is that the underlying cause is the regular or irregular energy of prayer. Like most human activities, it develops in phases. Periods of brightness are followed by duller periods. There are alternately times of encouragement and help, and times for developing our spiritual muscles. Dryness in prayer is a time for being faithful and staying with God; it is at this time that you learn to live by hope and faith and love for that which you do not yet see.

The second reason concerns discernment. The kind of boredom, anxiety and guilt that comes at one of these times of dryness can also be a sign that someone is trying to pray in the wrong way for them. It may be that they have set out to follow a model that does not suit them. It may be that they have changed within themselves and are growing into a new way of prayer.

The four ways of praying described in this chapter can be different stages in one person's spiritual development. It is not uncommon to begin with simple prayer in words, using a defined pattern of prayer. Later you may find the system too restricting and move into a more open, less wordy, approach to God through thinking, imagination, feelings or the will. The work of spiritual direction needs the sensitivity to notice the signs when someone ought to change and develop new ways of praying, or to support them as they come to terms with dryness.

Practicalities

What has been written so far will not be appropriate for everybody. To develop a pattern of prayer along the lines suggested may well be easier for people who can find the space in their lives for privacy and who are able to devote time to it during their day. It is not that you cannot pray unless you have leisure; rather, it is that your pattern of prayer has to be appropriate to what your life's demands allow.

For instance, the demands on a mother of a baby or small children, or on someone caring for an invalid at home, may well mean that prayer is a matter of a few scattered moments of turning attention to God rather than keeping a daily period of time offered as God's time.

Busy people and people whose life and work ask a lot of them may see their prayer as being offered in the things they do. It is a prayer of action, doing a job well for God's sake, or consciously offering the care you show someone else in need as a kind of intercession.

The Practice of the Presence of God (Hodder and Stoughton, 1982) is a short book by a lay brother in a monastery whose work was in the kitchens. In it he describes a way of prayer that is real to very many people whose lives are full of activity and have little space. It is a way of carrying God with you all the time, working as if consciously in his presence, being aware of the spiritual within the everyday.

The way to freedom from a conspiracy which is determined to keep work and Christian values apart is to develop a spirituality which sees life as an integrated whole. In a full understanding of God's creation there can be no parts which are separated off as areas in which Christianity has nothing important, or relevant, to say. No doubt most Christians would agree with this. Our task is to create a situation where divisions cannot creep in or, in places where they are established, to create such an atmosphere that divisions are seen to be contrived and artificial.

Pattern and rhythm

It can be helpful to have what is known as a 'Rule of Life'. This is a way of describing the pattern of praying and other aspects of discipleship which are the basis of a person's spirituality. It could include how much time is given to prayer daily or weekly; the pattern of Bible reading and of church worship; the proportion of money given away; time for family or relaxation; and other aspects of self-discipline that are appropriate. A Rule of Life like this is something to be worked out in discussion with someone else. The pattern should be sensible, feasible, and not wildly beyond your ability! There is no point in setting such high standards that they can never be achieved: that simply compounds feelings of guilt. Although it is right for many people to work out some kind of regular pattern like this, there are others who find it quite wrong for them; what seems a rigid structure reduces the spontaneity of their relationship with God.

Praying with the Bible

The stories in the Bible are a central resource for someone who is trying to pray and grow in prayer. But it is a very hard book to find your way around. Anyone who is acting as a guide to a new Christian needs to be able to help them into a creative use of the scriptures. This means, first of all, selection. Short passages, incidents, stories and sayings are the best material to work on in prayer. Slow, repetitive reading to draw out meanings is often more fruitful than covering a lot of ground. So it is useful to have a system to select by. There are the Sunday readings; there are booklets of selections and notes published by the Bible Reading Fellowship, Scripture Union and many other organizations. These cover a range of approaches to the Bible and are written for a range of different ages, abilities and interests.

Prayer is work; it is fun; it is shyness and sharing; it is a desperate plea for help and it is thanksgiving. More than anything else it becomes a conversation which takes place at different levels. It is the place where a disciple learns from, and gradually becomes a little more like, the Master.

References

Brother Lawrence, *The Practice of the Presence of God* (Hodder & Stoughton, 1982).

Westerhoff, John, *Building God's People in a Materialistic Society* (Seabury Press, 1983).

Wolters, Clifton (Tr), *The Cloud of Unknowing* (Penguin Classics, 1961).

EIGHT

❧

EASTER PEOPLE –
THE LIFE OF THE BAPTIZED

A young woman wrote:

It was Easter morning at dawn when I was baptized and confirmed. The service was very special, inasmuch as we went back in time to the early Church with all the richness and symbolism that it portrayed.

The bishop, clergy and people gathered at dawn to celebrate the Easter liturgy, Service of Light, baptism and confirmation. Easter is a time when we vividly recall the death and resurrection of our Lord. I often refer to that morning as my wedding day with all the excitement and nerves of the occasion. I arrived just before 5 a.m. The church was in complete darkness and the air was full of expectation as if something wonderful was about to happen – and of course it was.

Easter portrays just the start of our walk with our Lord. I was fully aware that my baptism and confirmation were just the beginning. I remember feeling very happy, a happiness that words cannot describe. I was floating like any bride on her wedding day and I knew he was happy too. I felt somehow he had given me so much more than I could ever give him in return. But he doesn't ask us to do that. All he wants is our love and I gave him that freely.

A year has gone by since the all-important 'Yes, I do' and it has been a year of change and adjustment. I have been getting to know my Lord a little better and it takes time. My journey continues.

The events of the first Easter mark a new beginning in the relationship between God and his people. There is a new hope and a new purpose. The same is true for someone who is baptized or confirmed or has made an important act of recommitment. The celebration of these sacraments points to a new beginning. The preparation for the big event has been completed, but it needs to be recognized as preparation for a new life and a new work as a member of the Church. It has been a time of equipping a man or woman to be sent into the world to work for the coming of the rule of God in the affairs of individuals, of communities and of nations.

The Anglican Liturgical Consultation meeting in 1991 at Toronto concluded:

> We see the catechumenal process affirming and celebrating the baptismal identity of the whole community. As people participate in the process, whether as enquirers, catechumens, candidates and initiates, or as sponsors, catechists and clergy, the baptism by which all are incorporated in the one body of Christ will be apprehended . . . Through the lens of baptism the people of God begin to see that lay ministry is important not simply because it allows an interested few to exercise their individual ministries, but because the ministry and mission of God in the church is the responsibility of all the baptised community.
>
> Baptism affirms the royal dignity of every Christian and their call and empowering for active ministry within the mission of the church . . . It makes the church a sign and instrument of the new world that God is establishing; it empowers Christians to strive for justice and peace within society. (Holeton, 1993)

We hope it has been clear from the earlier parts of this book that the purpose of 'Faith on the Way' is wider than simply to help adults to take part in the domestic events of the Church. It is all too easy for clergy and lay leaders to think in terms of people to do the jobs that need doing in the life of the Christian community. 'Wonderful! Here is Jim, who has just been confirmed. He's a motor mechanic, so let's get him to service the parish minibus' – as if the purpose of the Gospel was to make life easier for the group who believes! Far harder to grasp and far more important for the Kingdom of God is a response rather more like this: 'Wonderful! Here is Jim, who has just been confirmed. He's a motor mechanic. What difference does his being confirmed make to the way he does his job in the garage? What difference does his being confirmed make to God's activity among the people who manage and make up the staff at the garage? How can our church community help him and be associated with his ministry at work? What has he to tell the rest of us about his life there?'

Reflection leading to ministry

In the early Church the new Christians met with their bishop and other leaders after their baptism at Easter until Pentecost to reflect on what had happened to them in the baptismal water and in the breaking of the bread. They were helped to enter into the meaning of the sacraments and to make that meaning their own. They were invited to say for themselves, sometimes before the whole church, what difference their preparation and their entry into the full life of the church made to their lives.

The planning of 'Faith on the Way' in a parish must allow plenty of time for this stage in the growth of today's new Christians. The period before baptism or confirmation and the period after are different. Certainly in the preparation time there should be work together on what is likely to happen at baptism or confirmation and how it will affect the way a person looks at life; but that is all looking forward.

Once the event has happened, there is a change. Maggie stood up before the whole church and made her profession of faith. The church has celebrated with her a new beginning in the water of the font. The bishop has laid his hands on her head. Simon has invited members of his family who have scarcely ever attended church before to be with him at his confirmation; two friends from the firm where he works came too. It means that there are new situations to be lived through and new questions to be asked. Once you have made that sort of public commitment, you are stuck with it and you have to see where it may lead you. Once you have been accepted and empowered by God and the Church, you have a new kind of life to live and explore.

It is a time for the kind of reflection that gives plenty of space for people to sense what is important for them, to notice and deepen their feelings and awareness – in fact, it is a time to be open to hearing what God has to say to the new Christians about what he has done for them and what he asks from them. In comparison with the time of preparation leading up to baptism or confirmation, it has been described as a time for poetry rather than for prose.

The group should help the candidates to enter into what took place at their baptism or confirmation. Invite them to tell the story of what happened to them, what it felt like, how they feel about it now. It is important to value their insights, their embarrassment, their pleasure or their sense of the ridiculous. Those who were their sponsors will also have their story to tell about how it felt to stand by their friends and present them.

For the Kingdom

During the preparation time we would hope the group has worked together on the Church's mission and ministry in the world. They spent a lot of time deepening their understanding of the Christian Gospel, its effect on their own lives, and its implications for the society in which they live. They became aware of God's gifts to them and developed some ability to speak about them.

The period after baptism and confirmation is to help them to build on these earlier experiences with the strength that has come to them through their baptism or confirmation so that they are able to fulfil their own part within the whole mission and ministry of the Church.

'Mission' is the overall word for the Church being sent into the world. Within that sending there are three main aspects of mission. They interlock with each other, and the boundaries between them are fluid, but there are also distinctions between them.

Evangelism

The Church is sent into the world to proclaim the Good News of the coming of the Kingdom of God, the Good News of the salvation of the world through the coming, the death and the resurrection of Jesus Christ. It is the work of the Church, which means the work of the men and women who make up the Body of Christ, to be witnesses to the Gospel and to help others into faith in Christ. Christians are there to be agents of the Holy Spirit who is there before us.

The way to faith that we have worked through in this book tries to respond to this challenge. We are dealing with people to whom the Church has in one way or another announced the Good News. They are also people who, through the accompanied journey into faith, have been helped to open their hearts to that Good News and be changed by it.

In this period after their 'Easter', the purpose of the group is to work with them and see how the new Christians are to live out the calling to go and tell others. The story of Mary Magdalen at the tomb in St John's gospel gives a picture of this. Notice her movement away from being primarily a learner, someone who is dependent, towards being a person who is liberated to give to others and who, moreover, recognizes that she has been given authority to do so.

The style of the group during the period of learning and growing and during the final preparation helped the members to grow in confidence in speaking as well as listening. All the people taking part had the opportunity to develop confidence in sharing faith with one another. So it should not be too great a shock for the newly baptized or confirmed member of the Church to be asked to tell their story and talk about what they believe to another person.

The preparation for Christian initiation is a preparation for sharing in evangelism as one aspect of the whole work of the Church.

Service

At the height of the Christian Stewardship movement, when there was something like a blueprint for Stewardship Campaigns for parishes to follow, the section on 'Time and Talents' usually came after the big drive on money. As often as not, it fell flat on its face. In the same way that the 'money part' was generally seen as designed to provide cash for the church (however much that image failed to do justice to the underlying truths about people and their responsibility for God's gifts), so 'Time and Talents' came to be seen as asking what skills church people had to offer for the work of the congregation and the parish. Very rarely was the question asked 'How are you to offer the time and the talents which God has given you in your daily work?'

Many years ago Peter was chaplain in a television company, since closed down. He tells this story:

Two of the senior technicians had been moved by Christian Stewardship in their different churches. They recognized that the talents they had to offer God were their skills as, respectively, a sound supervisor and an engineer. Fired by their enthusiasm, we got together a working group which assembled a complete volunteer studio crew which was willing to work for the church at weekends when the studio was not in use. The company itself agreed to the free use of the studio. The trouble was that when we offered this remarkable facility to the church authorities, they had no idea how to use it.

Once lay people in the Church begin to play their full part in the formation of other lay Christians, then interest begins to focus more and more on the relationship between their faith and that area of their lives which takes up the working day and provides the money for them to buy the things they need. Work matters to men and women. Facing unemployment matters. Caring for a home and family matters. Living alone and coping with increasing disability matter. These are the situations where faith has to be worked out in practice. Of course, people will have worked on these things during the time of preparation; but in this period of reflection leading to ministry they are right in the forefront.

The church is a community called to serve the needs of the poor. St John's picture of Jesus washing the feet of his disciples at the Last Supper fills out the description of his calling in St Luke's story when he read from the book of Isaiah at the Nazareth synagogue service. All Christians are asked for generous giving of time and effort for other people, as well as proper giving of money. Often it is the newer members of the church who give an example to those of longer standing. During this time of reflection the group should consider what local or more distant needs are presented to the church and what part the new Christians are to play in meeting those needs. Their answers may challenge the rest of the congregation to a reawakening.

Body building

There is a real need for continuing growth and development of the Christian community if it is to be able to fulfil this commission to evangelize and to serve. New Christians and old alike need the chance to learn and to mature. They need the support and encouragement of one another and of their leaders, clergy and others.

So an element in the reflection leading to ministry is to see what part it is right for the new members to play within the life of the local church. There are all the possible ministries in Sunday services; there may be opportunities for taking part in one of the organizations of the parish; there are openings for practical work with people in their homes or around the church buildings.

It may be that within a fairly short time it is right to invite a new Christian to act as a companion to someone who is beginning their journey of faith, but this should not be too soon.

Closing down

Obviously the process in one sense never ends in this life. As human beings we are continually changing and regularly making new decisions. It is the same with the Christian life. If you are not open to growth and movement, you are dead. So one of the gifts that 'Faith on the Way' has to offer the Church is its emphasis on the importance of a conversion which is lifelong and on the duty of Christians to accompany one another along this journey.

You can't, or at least most people shouldn't, stay a beginner for ever. There comes a time when the initial stage of the journey is over and a new sort of life as a firmly belonging Christian takes over. Discipleship never closes down. As a companion of Jesus Christ you are always a learner; but in time you are also invited to become an apostle, someone who is sent out as part of his or her mission to the world. The period of reflection leading to ministry is about this transition.

When should the groups end? How should they finish? What continuing care should be available for new Christians? These are all very important questions, but there are no clear-cut, hard and fast answers.

The Roman Catholic bishops of the USA, in their introduction to the Rite of Christian Initiation of Adults, suggest that the preparation for baptism should last at least a full year, preferably fifteen months, and that there should be at least monthly meetings for new Christians over the year following their baptism to support them in their 'deeper Christian formation and incorporation into the full life of the Christian community'.

Individual needs will vary, and so will different groups. New

Christians should find the support they need from those who have accompanied them until now, but the clergy and other leaders should make sure that this is in fact happening.

Discernment is needed to find the right choices in particular situations. It may be right for a group that began as a preparation group for certain people to continue as, say, a house group within the life of the church. Or it may be better for the people in it to divide, to join existing groups, or help in the formation of new ones. The fellowship that grew over the months is not lost; friendships built along the journey of faith have a lasting quality.

Group work

Detailed suggestions for your own place and the actual men and women concerned should ideally grow naturally out of the individual and group experiences of the past months. The journey that we have followed in this book is only the first part of a lifelong pilgrimage in Christ and within the fellowship of his Body, the Church. We trust that it will lead all who follow into ever deeper awareness of his love and deeper commitment to his service. However, it may help to point to a few areas that the group can work on during this time after the baptism or confirmation of those who have been accompanied during their preparation.

- *Reflection.* Spend plenty of time simply recalling what has happened. Let everyone say for themselves what it was like to be baptized or confirmed, or to be there as a friend or companion, what it is like to receive Holy Communion. Give space to talk about awarenesses, perceptions and feelings of all sorts.

  Consider what the event means to the people who took part, what effect it has had on them, what difference it has made. Whether or not it was at the Easter season, see what the dying and rising with Christ means for the candidates. Help them to 'make it their own' and find appropriate ways of living it out.

  The readings for Easter Day and the following Sundays in Year A of the Common Lectionary provide a good resource for this kind of exploration. The First Letter of Peter in particular seems to be written as a kind of homily for the newly baptized of the early Church.

- *Ministry*. Look together at what practical changes follow from this reflection. Areas to notice include choices and relationships at home and at work; church life, both in its worship and in its social and practical life; involvement in issues of peace and justice and in the service of those in need locally and elsewhere; spirituality and the development of each person's relationship with God and its expression in life.
- *Church*. Ask what difference the work of the past months and in particular the baptism and confirmation of the candidates has made or should make to the life of the local church. What has the group to offer to the wider congregation? How should they make that offer known?

  Consider whether it would be right for those newly baptized and confirmed to speak about their journey and their experiences at one of the main Sunday services.
- *Closure*. Groups, especially groups that have the kind of strong fellowship that comes through following the journey together, develop a strong life of their own. The love and mutual support that characterize them mean that members often find it hard to stop meeting. People need help in dealing with the kind of bereavement that closure means. Some of the best parties have been the ones to mark the end of regular group sessions!

  Spend plenty of time looking at the ending of the life and work of the group. Make suitable arrangements for the continuing accompaniment of the new members over the months to come. Acknowledge the feelings the members have about not meeting regularly in the future. Fix a clear timetable for these final meetings. If it seems appropriate, organize a party to celebrate the beginning of a new stage in the journey.

Reference

Holeton, David R. (ed.), *Growing in Newness of Life: Christian Initiation in Anglicanism Today*, Papers from the Fourth Anglican Liturgical Consultation, Toronto 1991 (Anglican Book Centre, 1993).

༺❦༻

NINE

CELEBRATING THE JOURNEY:
THE RITES

PARISH EXPERIENCE in many different cultures has shown the power of the rites celebrating the stages on the enquirer's journey. This chapter outlines the ways in which rites may be used and suggests some forms of wording. The liturgies have several intentions and effects. On the individual plane they are an opportunity for enquirers to make a public statement about their growing Christian faith and what it means for them. For the congregation it is an opportunity to realize the responsibility which lies on the Christians in the pew to welcome and support with prayer people who want to join their community. In the rites and forms of prayer surrounding the baptism, confirmation or affirmation of baptismal faith of adults, the intention is to enable a congregation to share in the journey of faith of the individual candidates in the weeks before and after the baptism or its equivalent. As celebrations of the stages along the baptism journey, these liturgies have been shown to carry a blessing for those who take part. They are effective.

On the Way (Church House Publishing, 1995) gives this summary of the different aspects of the journey into Christian faith:

Five elements of Christian initiation

1. *Church* – Initiation calls the church
    to see itself as a baptised people
    to welcome and learn from the enquirer
    to be active in mission and service
    to expect the anointing of the Holy Spirit
    to walk with those seeking faith
    to stand with the despised and oppressed
    to look for the unity of God's people

2. *Welcome* – Enquirers need a welcome
    that is personal
    that is public
    that accepts their starting point
    that expects the presence of God in their lives
    that is willing to travel with them at their pace.

3. *Prayer* – Initiation involves prayer for enquirer and church
    to discern the presence of God
    to open up to the grace of God
    to support the process of change
    to discover the moments of decision
    to receive and recognise the gifts of God.

4. *The Way* – Discipleship means learning
    to worship with the church
    to grow in prayer
    to listen to the scriptures
    to serve our neighbour.

5. *Goal* – The goal of initiation is
    relationship with God the Trinity
    life and worship with the church
    service and witness in the world.

Sacramental rites should not be seen as isolated transactions but rather should be integrated with the social and spiritual processes which they represent. *Rites on the Way* (General Synod of the Church of England, 1998), is an interim report from the Liturgical Committee, giving an account of work in progress. It proposes a portfolio of rites and forms of prayer to surround the baptism and confirmation of adults. These are not offered as compulsory, nor yet as a set that have to be used in their entirety, but to support the spiritual journey of individuals and to enable the wider church community to support and learn from this journey.

A range of experience in the Church of England has expressed considerable interest in this process model of Christian Initiation. The Liturgical Commission has taken soundings and drawn on other models – particularly the Roman Catholic Rite of Christian Initiation of Adults.

This chapter offers rites and forms of prayer to support an

enquirer who wishes to enrol as a Learner in the Way of Christ. Many people, after an initial encounter with the church or impulse of faith, need the opportunity for a serious exploration of the Christian faith before they are ready to move on to baptism or some other sacramental affirmation of faith. Following the argument of *On the Way* the pattern identifies four dimensions to the Christian 'Way' in which Christ can be encountered and discipleship explored: worship; personal prayer; encounter with the scriptures in the community of faith; and service in the world.

Parishes and churches which have followed 'Faith on the Way' have often designed liturgies that suit the actual situation in the local church. Sometimes these have been very simple indeed. For instance, the Welcome might consist of a short introduction by the vicar or minister, followed by the candidates being invited to come forward with their sponsors to be introduced to the congregation, greeted with a right hand of fellowship, and commended for God's blessing in prayer. Others have used or adapted the RCIA or the American Episcopalian order with varying degrees of freedom. Now we have the beginning of liturgies officially designed and commended for use in the Church of England.

There are two ways in which these models can be used. They may be used whole as they stand, or they can be seen as a quarry from which ideas or whole sections may be taken by people designing liturgies for their own churches.

On the Way identifies the need to ground all Christians in certain formative texts that give shape to faith, prayer and discipleship, and urges that the Lord's Prayer, Jesus' Summary of the Law, the Apostles' Creed and the Beatitudes should form part of the initial formation of every Christian. Simple rites are offered, suitable either for informal, weekday use in small group meetings or for use in main Sunday services, in which these texts are presented to those who are exploring the Christian way.

These prayers and ceremonies are designed to focus the journey and to help people find their feet in a shared way of life. They consist of simple actions, prayers and readings from scripture. Jesus shows us that 'the Way' is personal – God touching real flesh-and-blood people, and also communal – God making himself present in a community of people. They are intended to speak to the person who wants to learn the way of Christ and to the community of the

Church which God intends to support them and to learn with them.

Although 'the Way' is open to all and leads to a deeper understanding of life, it is not always easy. The cost may be high and the twists and turns unpredictable. Although every person's journey is unique, it need not – perhaps cannot – be made alone. The learner on the road has three places to turn, three sources of strength and understanding. The first is Jesus the fellow-traveller, often unrecognized, the image and agent of God, who makes himself known to us on the journey as well as in the life of the church. The second is the church, the community of those who follow 'the Way'. The third is the Bible, the sacred writings that open God's ways to us, that have the power to make us wise and lead us to salvation through faith in Jesus Christ.

It is the privilege and calling of the church as the people of God and the sign of Christ to welcome and support those who are learning 'the Way', to pray for them and to walk with them. Such people are a sign to the church of its own calling. It must welcome them as examples and teachers, as those who will bring a glimpse of God that no one else can make known. It must see them as bearers of hope and be willing to share with them 'the Way' that it is itself discovering. The church must be a companion to those learning the way of Christ; it will therefore also provide them with companions as well as teachers, with sponsors as well as instructors.

There is more to exploring 'Faith on the Way' than learning certain facts about the past or celebrating the love and grace of God for each person. Discipleship means learning a way of life. The Christian life involves action and will take the disciple into unfamiliar territory. There are ways of worship and belonging to be learned; values and priorities to be reviewed; patterns of prayer and service to be established. It will involve learning to be at home in the church and to be a sign of God's Kingdom in the world. Exploring 'the Way' includes learning about worship with the church; the life of prayer; listening to God through the Bible; and serving your neighbour in the world.

Baptism is both a beginning and a goal in the Christian life. The baptism of Jesus marked the arrival in human history of hopes long desired: the presence of God among us, the beginning of the reign of God destroying evil and restoring our humanity. It made visible the life of the Trinity and revealed the coming Kingdom of God. For Jesus it represented not simply a beginning but a consecration to God's way of salvation. Again, for Christians baptism is not simply a beginning: it is a mark of ownership and a sign of our calling. It is a seal or stamp that declares who we are and sets the style and shape of the life to which we are called. The Baptism Service, following the New Testament, uses many rich images to draw out the identity, dignity and vocation that God gives us through baptism.

Exploring the imagery and implications of baptism is an important part of the way of Christ. Baptism is not something to be left behind but a sign to be entered into at each stage of our journey of faith. Those who are exploring the way of Christ for the first time set their feet on a path that God intends to lead to baptism, the sign of the Kingdom of God. There is a sense in which these liturgies celebrating stages on the journey are in fact stages of the celebration of baptism. Indeed, in the French church the work of the catechumenate is referred to as 'Baptism by Stages'.

Many of the people who follow 'Faith on the Way' as enquirers will be candidates for confirmation, having been christened as babies. However, the proportion of those who are not baptized is going to increase as the years go on, and there is already a significant number in adult classes who are preparing for their baptism.

For those who have been baptized every stage of life is an opportunity to re-appropriate this sign – to enter again into the identity and calling that baptism signifies. This is true for children growing up in the life of the church, for teenagers establishing their own identity, for adults affirming their baptismal faith for themselves or beginning to explore this faith for the first time. With confirmation and with affirmation of baptismal faith we are offered ways of entering again into our baptism.

The difference between candidates for baptism and candidates for confirmation needs to be recognized in the design and celebration of the liturgies marking stages along the way. In baptism, a person has joined the Church: he or she is already a member. The words of the service for someone preparing for confirmation must give full value to this.

The Service of Welcome

The purpose of the service is to mark the start of a person's committed journey, the first signs of their Christian faith, and their joining a group to begin a course that may lead to baptism, confirmation or the affirmation of their baptismal vows. It is intended for those who, after an initial exploration of the Christian faith, wish to investigate and learn the Christian way within the context of the life of the people of God. It is not intended for initial enquirers. It expresses the congregation's welcome to enquirers or new members. The church hears the request that an enquirer makes and accepts it. The enquirer is given a sign of belonging, either the sign of the cross, a copy of the scriptures or the gospels. There is prayer for them.

The enquirers should agree with the minister on a member of the church to be their companion and supporter and to act as their sponsor. Sponsors may be commissioned for their ministry with the enquirers.

The congregation needs to be encouraged by careful teaching to support and pray for them, and to see them as examples.

The following form may be used to welcome an enquirer as a learner in the way of Christ. It may be included in any form of public worship. It may be placed towards the beginning of the service as part of the introduction, or before or after the prayers. At a Eucharist it may be used at the church door, before the collect, after the sermon, before the peace, or after communion. If it takes place at the very beginning of the service it can be a sign of enquirers being welcomed to the church as it learns from the Ministry of the Word. Placing it after the sermon gives the opportunity for preaching about the event and its importance before it happens. The form may be adapted as seems appropriate or additional forms of symbolic action included. It will be helpful for members of the congregation to be involved in planning the service.

Where an enquirer has been baptized, the second form is used at the signing with the cross. Where so wished, pure olive oil blessed for this purpose by the bishop may be used at the signing with the cross.

It is best if there is actual movement of people through the building, bringing the new members in from outside the church, from the porch or from the back of the church to the front, introducing them to the congregation and then accepting them into their place as part of the community.

Their sponsors should stand and move with the enquirers throughout the service. In churches with sound amplification, care should be taken that the different times of dialogue are heard by the whole church.

Suitable music should be chosen for appropriate points in the rite.

The first six liturgies which follow are suggestions which appear in *Rites on the Way*.[1]

Welcoming an Enquirer as a Learner in the Way of Christ
(*Rites on the Way*, Church House Publishing, 1998)

The minister may introduce the welcome in these or similar words:

> Today it is our joy and privilege to welcome *N* and *N*
> as learners in the way of Christ.
> They are among us as a sign of the discipleship to
> which we are all called.

The minister invites the enquirer(s) to come and stand before the people.
They and their sponsor(s) come forward. The sponsor may introduce
them by name. The minister says:

> (*N* and *N*/friends). We thank God for his presence in
> your life/lives and for the grace that has brought you
> here today. We welcome you.
> What is it that you seek?

The enquirer may reply in his or her own words or may say one of the fol-
lowing:

> To explore the Christian faith.
> To learn the way of Christ.

One of the following may be used:

Minister   God is not far from each one of us.
              He has created us to feel after him and find him.
              The ancient promise stands: when we seek God, we
              will find him, if we seek him with all our heart.

Or

Minister   Jesus has opened for us the way to the Father.
              Seek and you will find. Knock, and the door will be
              opened to you.

*The minister may pray in silence with each enquirer and may also pray
in his/her own words.*
The sponsor and others may join in this action.
*After all have been prayed with, the minister says this or a similar prayer.
It may be said over each candidate or once over the whole group:*

> God of life, guide N/these servants by your wisdom
> and surround them with your love.
> Deepen their knowledge and love of Christ and set
> their feet on the way that leads to life.
> May your people uphold them in love, find in them a
> sign of hope, and learn with them the way of Christ.
> Amen.

*The minister then addresses each candidate separately or the group
together:*

> Will you receive the sign of the cross as a mark of
> Christ's love, power and protection as you explore his
> way?

Enquirer   I will.

*A minister signs the candidate with the sign of the cross. The sponsor may
also sign their candidate. The president says:*

> N. Receive the sign of the cross, the sign of Christ's
> love and power.
> May his Spirit be your guide and protector.

[Where a candidate is already baptised, these words are used:

> N. God who has called you is faithful and in your
> baptism claimed you as his own.
> Receive the sign of the cross; may the love and power
> of Christ be with you.]

*The candidate is handed a copy of the scriptures or of a Gospel with the
following words:*

Seek in this book new life in Christ, who is the Word
of God and the hope of the world.

The minister may address the sponsors:

As we have welcomed *N*/these enquirers, so will you
accompany them on the journey of faith, supporting
them with friendship, love and prayer?

Sponsors   With the help of God, we will.

The minister addresses the congregation:

People of God, We have welcomed *N*/these enquirers
in the love and hope of Christ. Will you support and
pray for them, and learn with them the way of Christ?

All   With the help of God, we will.

Presentations of the Four Core Texts
(*Rites on the Way*, Church House Publishing, 1998)

Some parishes follow the pattern of the early Church and celebrate
other occasions along the journey. *On the Way* proposes that all
baptized Christians should be encouraged to make four texts their
own in order to give shape to their discipleship: the Summary of the
Law, the Lord's Prayer, the Apostles' Creed, and the Beatitudes.
There is no particular time in the journey of faith when these texts
should be delivered to those on this journey. It may be on certain
Sundays in the final preparation period, or at points in the time of
learning and growing when the subjects in the core texts have been
specifically discussed. What follow are forms of service which could
be used in public worship or in smaller group meetings for the
handing over of these core texts.

There are also powerful Lenten liturgies of self-examination, penitence and special prayer, which form part of the final preparation of
candidates for baptism or confirmation at Easter. Forms of service for
these can be found in books listed in Chapter 11.

Presentation of Jesus' Summary of the Law

One of the following or other readings may be used:
Exodus 20:1–18; Leviticus 19:9–18; Romans 8:1–4; Romans 13:8–10; Galatians 5:13–14; Mark 12:28–34.

One of the following psalms may be used:
Psalm 1; 15; 119:9–16; 119:97–104.

At a suitable place in the service, possibly after the sermon and in place of the creed, the minister addresses those who are exploring for themselves the Christian way:

> Dear friends, listen carefully to the words that Jesus gave us as a summary of the law. These few words help us understand how we are to live as human beings in God's world. They are given not to condemn us but to show how by the grace of God we may live as free people reflecting the goodness and love of God.

The Summary of the Law is then read to the assembly by two members of the congregation.

Minister   If we live by the Spirit,
Candidates   let us also walk by the Spirit.

The minister says:

> Let us pray.
> Lord, you have taught us that all our doings without love are nothing worth: send your Holy Spirit and pour into our hearts that most excellent gift of love, the true bond of peace and of all virtues, without which whoever lives is counted dead before you. Grant this for your only Son Jesus Christ's sake. Amen.

Presentation of the Lord's Prayer

One of the following or other readings may be used:
1 Kings 8:27–30; Hosea 11:1–4; Romans 8:14–17, 26, 27; Galatians
4:4–7; Matthew 6:7–13; Luke 11:1–4.

One of the following psalms may be used:
Psalm 23; 103:6–18.

*At a suitable place in the service, possibly after the sermon and in place of
the creed, the minister addresses those who are exploring for themselves
the Christian way:*

> Dear friends, listen carefully to the prayer that Jesus
> taught his disciples. It is given to us as a pattern for our
> praying as well as a prayer that we can make our own.
> It teaches us that heaven is open to our prayer and that
> the world is open to the gracious working of God.

*The Lord's Prayer is then read to the assembly by a member of the congre-
gation.*

Minister   Eternal life is to know God as Father
Candidates   and to know Jesus Christ whom he has sent.

The minister says:

> Let us pray.
> Almighty and everlasting God, you are always more
> ready to hear than we to pray and to give more than
> either we desire or deserve: pour down upon us the
> abundance of your mercy, forgiving us those things of
> which our conscience is afraid and giving us those
> good things which we are not worthy to ask but
> through the merits and mediation of Jesus Christ your
> Son our Lord. Amen.

Presentation of the Apostles' Creed

One of the following or other readings may be used:
Deuteronomy 6:1–7; Deuteronomy 26:1–10; Romans 10:8–13; 1 Timothy 6:11–16; 2 Timothy 1:8–14; Matthew 16:13–18; John 12:44–50.

One of the following psalms may be used:
Psalm 78:1–7; 145:1–9.

At a suitable place in the service, possibly after the sermon and in place of the creed, the minister addresses those who are exploring for themselves the Christian way:

> Dear friends, listen carefully to this ancient text which the Church calls the Apostles' Creed. It was formed in the earliest centuries in the celebration of baptism. It teaches us the shape of Christian belief about God and also gives us a framework through which to understand the history of the world. Follow the pattern of sound teaching and live by the faith and love which are ours in Christ Jesus.

The Apostles' Creed is then read to the congregation by three or four members of the congregation.

Minister	Follow the pattern of sound teaching.
Candidates	Live by the faith and love that are ours in Christ Jesus.

The minister says:

> Let us pray.
> Most Merciful God, who by the death and resurrection of your Son Jesus Christ delivered and saved the world: grant that by faith in him who suffered on the cross we may triumph in the power of his victory; through Jesus Christ your Son our Lord. Amen.

Presentation of the Beatitudes

One of the following or other readings may be used:
Isaiah 2:2–4; Isaiah 11:1–10; Ephesians 3:7–13; 1 John 3:1–3;
Revelation 21:22–27; Mark 4:30–32.

One of the following psalms may be used:
Psalm 72:1–14; 87; 122.

*At a suitable place in the service, possibly after the sermon and in place of
the creed, the minister addresses those who are exploring for themselves
the Christian way:*

> Dear friends, listen carefully to these words from the
> Sermon on the Mount. In them Jesus gives us a vision
> of a transformed world and of the qualities and
> discipleship which lead towards that transformation.

*The Beatitudes are then read to the assembly by two or three members of
the congregation.*

Minister	The creation itself will be set free from its bondage to decay
Candidates	and obtain the glorious liberty of the children of God. In this hope we are saved.

The Minister says:

> Let us pray.
> Almighty God, who alone can bring order to the
> unruly wills and passions of sinful humanity: give your
> people grace so to love what you command and to
> desire what you promise, that, among the changes of
> this world, our hearts may surely there be fixed where
> true joys are to be found; through Jesus Christ our
> Lord. Amen.

Celebration of God's Call

This service, against the background of a belief in a God who chooses and calls his people, makes formal and celebrates the Church's invitation and the enquirer's readiness for baptism, confirmation or the affirmation of baptismal vows. It expresses the process of discernment that has already taken place among the people responsible, and affirms the congregation's support.

Where the confirmation is not to take place in the candidates' church, this rite can be adapted to commend them for confirmation at another centre.

In the parish Eucharist, the rite takes place after the sermon. It may form the theme for a Family Service, Morning or Evening Prayer in churches where the Eucharist is not the main Sunday service.

At the time of writing the Church of England Liturgical Commission is still working on the liturgy for this stage in the journey of Christian Initiation. So we offer here two orders as examples. The first is one which has been designed and used by parishes in England. The second has been developed by a co-operative inter-church process involving three Lutheran churches in North America.[2]

A Suggested Order for 'God's Call'

After the sermon the congregation stands.

President   The Lord be with you.
Congregation And also with you.

A group leader says:

> Our friends are completing their time of preparation. They have been strengthened by God's grace and supported by this community's example and prayers. They come today to ask that they may soon be allowed to enter into the full sacramental life of the Church.

President   The life of faith in Jesus Christ is a journey of discovery. At the Service of Welcome we rejoiced with *N* and *N* and supported them with our prayers as they entered a new stage on their journey. Today we celebrate with them as they commit themselves to accept their responsibility within the priesthood of all believers and approach baptism or confirmation. We pray for them, their sponsors and ourselves that we may all be worthy of our calling. Almighty God, by whose grace alone we are accepted and called to your service: strengthen us by your Holy Spirit and make us worthy of our calling; through Jesus Christ our Lord. Amen.

The president then invites the candidates and sponsors to come forward.

President	These people have asked to be admitted into the full sacramental life of the Church. For a long time they have heard the word of Christ and have been trying to live in his way. Those who know them judge them to be sincere in their desire. I now ask the sponsors to affirm their support. You have accompanied *N* on his/her journey. Do you believe that he/she is ready to make this commitment?
Sponsor	(A personal reply is given.)
President	Are you willing to make [or renew] your baptism commitment in Christ?
Candidate	I am.
President	Do you agree that these candidates should go forward for baptism and confirmation?
Congregation	We do.
President	(*to each candidate*) *N*, you have been chosen and called to enter into the fullness of the Christian mysteries.
Candidate	Thanks be to God.
President	(*addressing the candidates*) Now it is your duty and ours to ask the help of God. He is always faithful to those he calls. (*addressing the sponsors*) These people have been entrusted to you in the Lord. By your loving care and example, go on helping them and praying for them as they look forward to receiving the sacraments of salvation.

May the Lord bless you, protect you from all evil and guide you in his way.

A short litany is said.

Enrolment of Candidates for Baptism
(*Welcome to Christ: Lutheran Rites for the Catechumenate*, Augsburg Fortress, 1997)

The enrolment of candidates for baptism at the Vigil of Easter normally takes place during the principal service of the congregation the First Sunday in Lent. When baptism takes place at another time, enrolment should precede it by several weeks.

If the names of candidates for baptism are to be written in a book as part of the rite, a large and beautiful book lies open at a place in the midst of the congregation where it can be easily seen and used. The book may be placed near the list of those for whom the congregation prays each time it gathers.

Presentation of candidates
A catechist presents the candidates with these or similar words:

These persons desire to make public their intention to be baptized at the coming festival of Our Lord's death and resurrection.

The presiding minister asks the candidates:

By God's grace you have been drawn to this congregation. You have heard the word of God and prayed with us. Do you desire to be baptized?

Each candidate responds:

I do.

The presiding Minister addresses the sponsors with these or similar words:

> You have been companions to these women and men
> in their journey of faith. Have they been faithful in
> hearing the word of God and in receiving it as the
> pattern for their lives?

Response: Yes, by the grace of God.

The minister addresses the congregation with these or similar words:

> People of God, as you journey through Lent, will you
> support these persons, chosen by God, through your
> prayer, presence, and example? As you observe the dis-
> ciplines of Lent, will you be for them a community of
> love and growth in God's grace?

Response: We will, and we ask God to help us.

> The following persons are candidates for baptism:
> [names]

> We welcome you to this time of preparation for
> baptism at Easter.

Enrolment of names

*A sponsor or catechist may write the name of each person to be baptized
in the congregation's book, or the candidate may sign his or her own name
in the book while a catechist reads out each name for the congregation to
hear.*

*After each name is read aloud, and while the names are inscribed in the
book one of the following or another response may be sung:*

> Lord Jesus, you call your own by name, and lead them
> to the waters of life.

Or

> God calls you to be one with Jesus Christ our Lord.

A catechism may be presented to each candidate.

Blessing of the candidates

The presiding minister continues with these or similar words:

The Lord be with you.

Response: And also with you.

Presiding   Let us pray.
Minister: Merciful and most high God, creator and life-giver of
all that is,
you have called all people from darkness into light,
from error into truth, from death into life.
We ask you: grant grace to [names] and bless them.
Raise them by your Spirit.
Revive them by your word.
Form them by your hand.
Bring them to the water of life and to the bread and
cup of blessing,
that with all your people they may bear witness to your
grace
and praise you for ever through Jesus Christ our Lord.
Amen.

The assisting minister concludes with these or similar words:

Journey with us now through Lent as we prepare
for the festival of our Lord's death and resurrection.
May God bring you in peace and joy to the day of your
baptism
and to fullness of life in Christ.
Amen.

*The candidates and sponsors return to their places. The congregation may
sing one of the following or another response:*

May the God of all grace who has called you to glory
support you and make you strong.

Or

> Blessed be God who chose you in Christ. Live in love
> as Christ loved us.

Baptism, confirmation and Eucharist

The liturgy for the baptism of adults with confirmation and the
Eucharist is to be found in *Common Worship: Initiation Services. Lent,
Holy Week and Easter* provides an order for the Easter Vigil. Both
these can be developed and adapted within the limits given so that
the celebration makes a fitting climax to the journey of initiation that
the candidates have followed.

The Anglican *Initiation Services* makes provision for baptisms at
Easter, All Saints and Epiphany as well as at other times under a
'General' provision.

Affirmation of Baptismal Faith

People who have already been baptized and confirmed when much
younger and have come by 'the Way' to a renewed adult faith have
the opportunity to celebrate the Affirmation of Baptismal Faith at
the same service as their companions are confirmed. Again, this is
found in *Initiation Services* and should be celebrated with imagination and relevance to the people taking part.

Without in any sense making the event a 're-baptism', it is possible
to use water as a sign in this renewal. Either the person may be sprin-
kled or they may use water themselves. Anointing with oil is an
ancient sign used by the early Church at different points along the
enquirer's journey. The scented Oil of Chrism in particular has its use
with those who are newly baptized and those who are renewing their
vows.

Worksheet 5A: Planning the Service of Welcome

Preparation
Ensure that the people who need to be are invited to the meeting or kept informed of decisions. These may include, among others, the clergy, the organist, servers, churchwardens, group leaders and sponsors.

Task
- Decide the order of service and arrange photocopying if necessary.
- Work out the movements of people in the service.
- Choose the music.
- Decide if you need a rehearsal for sponsors and make arrangements accordingly.

Worksheet 5B: Planning the Celebration of God's Call

1. Discernment
At an appropriate review session clergy and lay leaders should pray for and talk about the people who are in preparation for baptism and confirmation.

Notice how each feels about the readiness or otherwise of the candidates to be presented for initiation.

Spend time discussing people about whom there are questions. Decide how to approach them before coming to final conclusions.

Try to be clear about the different responsibilities of the individual candidates concerned, the leaders of the groups and the parish clergy in this discernment.

2. Service preparation
- Decide who are the appropriate people to be involved in preparation and who has to be kept informed.

- Decide on the form of service and arrange photocopying if necessary.
- Decide on the method of presentation of the candidates. Is it to be formal or informal?
- Decide on what movements are to take place and what symbols are to be used.

References

On the Way: Towards an Integrated Approach to Christian Initiation (Church House Publishing, 1995).

Rites on the Way; Work in Progress, A Paper from the Liturgical Commission, GS Misc 530 (Church House Publishing, 1998).

Welcome to Christ: Lutheran Rites for the Catechumenate (Augsburg Fortress, 1997).

Notes

1   Extracts from *Rites on the Way: Work in Progress* (GS Misc 530, July 1998) are copyright © The Central Board of Finance of the Church of England, 1998; The Archbishops' Council, 1999, and are reproduced by permission.

2   Reprinted by permission from *Welcome to Christ: Lutheran Rites for the Catechumenate*, copyright © 1997, Augsburg Fortress.

TEN

MYSTAGOGIA!

ONE OF THE HARDEST WORDS to get into the lifeblood of 'Faith on the Way' has been the word, but not the concept, of *mystagogia*. In the early Church this term was used to describe the life of the baptized as they grew in faith and were nourished by the sacraments, particularly in the week after Easter as they were 'led into the mystery' of the Baptism and Eucharist they had just experienced.

In this chapter we need to do some *mystagogia* for ourselves, reflecting on the progress, achievements and frustrations of our work in 'Faith on the Way' over more than thirty years. What has it been like to be converts ourselves to this way of working? What has it been like to live in the community of those who believe in it? What has it been like to accompany others, and what has it been like to live in a church where this way is seen as one among many?

We need to look at how the movement has developed in the United Kingdom and why it has taken its particular shape. We have to celebrate the great achievement of ecumenical co-operation with our colleagues in the Roman Catholic Church who have been implementing and developing the Rite of Christian Initiation of Adults over a similar time. We need to tell the story of work with colleagues, often in pioneering situations, in different parts of the world. We have to look at why what has been known as the Adult Catechumenate did not become an organization with a network and wide range of resources and publications. In a final harvesting we want to suggest what 'Faith on the Way' is offering, and can offer in a more developed way, to the growth and development of the Christian faith for those inside and on the fringes of the Church.

The British story

It was Peter Ball's first meeting with Jim Cranswick in 1969 that began our discovery of the Catechumenate. Together with his parishioners at St Nicholas, Shepperton, among them one of the early group leaders, Sandy Hayter, he began to develop work along these lines. Christopher Bryan, who was then Director of Education and Community in the Diocese of London, gave encouragement. The partnership of Peter Ball and Malcolm Grundy, along with many others, began when Malcolm took over from Christopher early in 1980. Together they ran consultations and study days, at first in London, and then in many other parts of Britain. The Adult Catechumenate Network was born at that time, with a membership of clergy and lay people who were beginning to use the method in their parishes.

A newsletter was published and Peter's books began to come out – *Journey into Faith* in 1984; *Adult Believing: a Guide to the Christian Initiation of Adults* in 1988 and *Adult Way to Faith* in 1992. Grove Booklets published Malcolm Grundy's *Evangelization through the Adult Catechumenate* in 1991. The Church of England began to take an interest in this movement through several of its Boards and Councils. The work did not fit into any one category. Because it was about preparing adults for baptism and confirmation, and contained its own initiation rites, it came within the work of the Liturgical Commission. The methods of accompanying adults into a deeper faith used many contemporary styles of adult learning; consequently there was interest from the Board of Education. Equally significant was the work of bringing adults to faith and into the life of the Church, where the Board of Mission took an active interest.

In a Decade of Evangelism this was a piece of imaginative adult evangelization which required attention and a rigorous critique. The House of Bishops commissioned a working party to study faith development methods under the Chairmanship of the Bishop of St Edmundsbury and Ipswich. Their report was published in 1995 as *On the Way* (Church House Publishing). Even though there was an interested readership and considerable discussion within dioceses, it was never brought for debate in the Church of England's General Synod.

Ecumenical co-operation

The Second Vatican Council of the Roman Catholic Church in 1963 gave great encouragement to the development of the catechumenate. With the *Constitution on the Sacred Liturgy* the Council set in motion the revision of the rite of baptism of adults and decreed that the catechumenate for adults be restored. The Catholic Church had much experience of the use of catechists in developing countries where there were not enough priests.

Lay people with a basic training prepared enquirers and new converts for baptism. They were also seen as the mainstay of many local Christian groups. The early Church's method of preparing new Christians was brought into contemporary use.

In the modern Roman Catholic Church various strands of the catechumenate developed, not all of them orthodox. Close co-operation sprang up between those engaged in Anglican and Catholic work in London. The RCIA office for the Archdiocese of Westminster in Kensington Square and the Education and Community Department's Offices of the Diocese of London at St Andrew's, Holborn, became twin centres of influence and activity. Anglican and Catholic colleagues began to meet with others from across the country in both formal and informal ways.

The European network

The European churches have worked together in particularly constructive ways throughout this century. Ecumenical co-operation during the 1930s led to significant friendships and exchanges of information during the Second World War and afterwards. When the concept of Europe as a new economic unit began to emerge in the 1950s, church groupings became established to relate to these structures. In the world of adult education the Roman Catholic Church formed a European network which was soon followed by one for the Protestant churches.

Anglicans were represented early in the development of the European Conference on the catechumenate. In due course they were joined by Catholics from Britain to form a joint delegation to European meetings. The 2001 European Conference in Leeds under the title 'Pearls of Great Price; Stories from the Threshold' is the fruit of joint planning by Roman Catholics and Anglicans.

A particularly pleasing association has developed over twenty years with the Church of Sweden. From contacts made by Malcolm and Peter, courses have been held in London and in many dioceses in Sweden to promote 'Faith on the Way'. Significant contributions have been made by individuals. The Revd Anders Alberius from the Diocese of Växjö, now Director of the Bible Society of Sweden, was an early advocate. He arranged to have Malcolm's book translated into Swedish by his journalist brother. He was succeeded as leader of the Swedish network by the Revd Karl-Gunnar Ellverson, a faculty member at the Pastoral Institute in Uppsala. Many dioceses appointed specialists to develop these working methods, among them the Revd Elizabeth Lindow in Växjö and Karen Lindström in Luleå. In a church which had little experience of adult members of congregations sharing faith, or volunteering in any way, this has been an important agent of regeneration. Sweden now has its own body of writing and training materials.

Other parts of the world

Close links have also been maintained with both Episcopalians and Catholics in America and Canada, where the National Forum on the Catechumenate largely serves Catholics and the NAAC's many other denominations. The same is true of Australia and New Zealand, where Peter has taken a leading part in local and national training events.

A first worldwide symposium was held at Lyon in 1993 with participants from every continent, and a second is planned to take place in the USA in 2002.

Experience and frustration in Britain

For all the 'middle years' of our work we could not help wondering why the network did not develop into a really popular movement with widespread active membership. Was it because we lacked the entrepreneurial drive and financial backing to promote our work really vigorously? That may be the case, but it did not explain why the hundreds of parishes and congregations who heard about 'Faith on the Way' on our courses and training days accepted some of its influences, but did not fully continue with this type of initiation work.

Was it because we refused to publish handbooks, manuals, work-sheets or even a video to help with promotion and dissemination? This is a possible practical answer. The Network did go through a phase when we felt that producing materials and promotion in the manner of Alpha or Emmaus was the route which we should take. There were occasions when we thought that they had stolen our clothes! However, nothing of what other people were producing fitted in with our understanding of the process involved in the way our groups worked.

We were also aware that the mood and the evangelistic style of the churches had changed. In the 1960s, when we began, it was thought that a rigorous examination of the essentials of the faith would bring new believers to faith and into the Church. We moved through the 1970s where our educational methods were close to those which were influential in training work. Group work was very much the way to operate, however badly it was done, and with whatever damaging consequences. The 1980s were a time of crisis in many churches when money and vocations seemed to be drying up and when congregations were drained by the work of sheer survival. We carried on with our methods into the 1990s where a very different mood prevailed.

With a population who knew very little of the Christian story, the prevailing mood was one of needing to tell the basics of the faith. Our slow, faith-sharing approach, accompanying enquirers at their own pace and working with the questions they ask along the way, was out of fashion. Training materials, courses and evangelistic pro-grammes returned to telling enquirers about the faith, giving them information and an early sense of secure certainty before questions of reflection, or even doubt, could begin to surface.

A shared discovery

Formal conversations with our Roman Catholic colleagues have given us a time of mature, objective reflection. We found that they were experiencing very much the same response within their own church. Parishes which were using the RCIA. were, in the main, not entering into the 'spirit' of the process. There was a great desire to find answers in books. The structure of the RCIA was there without its living content. Like us, they were beginning to come to terms with their Catholic Alpha!

What our joint conversations have helped us to see is that what we have developed is not one course, one way of working, among many. What we have is a basic understanding of the methodology and experience of enquirers coming to faith through an accompanied journey. We recognize how adults learn and what human and material resources are needed to allow this process to flourish. We have pioneered the development of a series of Rites which allows those coming into the Church to celebrate the stages of their spiritual journey. We have shared experience of using the symbolism of light, water, colour and scent in these Rites. We went on to surprise ourselves in our shared exploration of this strange Greek word *mystagogia*, as newly initiated Christians share with us the continuing challenge of living a life in the world, supported by a commitment to the Church.

A bold discovery

Reflection on our experience has enabled us to come to quite a different conclusion from that which the evidence of our work might have suggested. On the face of it we spent many years encouraging a way of welcoming adults into the community of faith with no national movement to show for it. We have had our work evaluated and affirmed by the Bishops of the Church of England, but none of them had put any human resources into its development in their dioceses. We have seen new published courses emerge and overtake our advocacy.

Nevertheless, our reflection has led us to conclude that our frustration might have come because we were looking in the wrong places for what we had achieved.

How congregations behave

What you have been able to read in the central chapters of this book about 'Faith on the Way' is the series of key characteristics which any growing congregation will have. We have developed them from our understanding of how adults grow in faith and learn about Chris-

tianity. We use the methods of the first Christians in the early centuries. Although 2,000 years span the story of how people come to
faith, we are not engaged in ecclesiastical archaeology. These are
living methods which allow discoveries to be made about a faith for
today.

The catechumenate is not a course; it is a way of life for any Christian community which has life in it. Our methods express a
sensitivity in a community which will help people to faith. We
commend them to you as a way of welcoming and accompanying
adults on the way of faith. We commend them also as the way in
which the life of a congregation and its ministers can be renewed.
This is the work of the Holy Spirit giving birth and life to a faith
which will grow and develop as Christians journey together and tell
their stories to one another. To many in a local church which is alive,
it will seem like enlightened common sense. To those in congregations which have lost their way, it can be a signpost towards new life.

A grid for every church

Neither Peter nor Malcolm have confined their work to the development of 'Faith on the Way', though they would both say that their
other work in faith development and analysis is contained within it.

We both have an early background in the work of Industrial
Mission. Peter has a ministry as a spiritual director and is the author
of an examination of the lives of other directors, *Journey into Truth:
Spiritual Direction in the Anglican Tradition* (1996). Malcolm is well
known for his consultations on the development of congregations;
he has put together his own research and that of many others in
Understanding Congregations (1998). The basic way of looking at the
life of a Christian community, using the discoveries of reflection
about 'Faith on the Way' unfolds in a simple but direct way. We have
come to see that it contains the four characteristics which every congregation needs to have in some measure. There will not be an equal
balance, and at different times a congregation will need to give these
facets different emphases. If any if these are missing there will be a
serious imbalance which will, in the end, bring a weakening of congregational life.

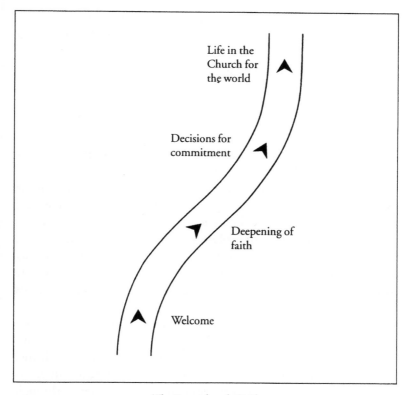

Life in the
Church for
the world

Decisions for
commitment

Deepening of
faith

Welcome

The Everychurch Grid

Our discovery unpacked

We often sense that something is missing in the life of our local
Christian community, or of a church that we visit. Here is a way to
find what that missing element might be. Let us call the necessary
parts of a church with life the Everychurch Grid.

- *Welcome:* There have to be a number of different ways in which
  enquirers can be welcomed into the life of a congregation.
- *Deepening of faith:* There has to be, within the life of a congregation, a series of ways in which faith can be explored and even
  discovered anew.
- *Decision for commitment:* At certain times in the life of an individual, or in the life of a congregation, decisions about faith and
  lifestyle have to be made. There has to be a 'cutting edge' to our
  faith.

- *Life in the church:* In order to sustain a living faith within a community of believers, there have to be ways in which that life can be reviewed. Sometimes a 'survival kit' for life within the church needs to be devised. The purpose of the kit is to enable renewed discipleship in the world.

The marks of 'Faith on the Way'

These are just a slight adaptation and development of the characteristics and stages of 'Faith on the Way'.

On very many occasions when we have been setting 'Faith on the Way' out to clergy and congregations, they have said, 'But we are doing this already.' The enlightened community with a reasonably secure priest is not afraid to explore new things. Parishes like that are, in the main, the ones who have invited us to talk. They are already 'on the way' to congregational development and renewed priestly formation. We were indeed exchanging with such congregations ideas of good practice within church life.

The important difference is that we are putting this experience into a systematic form. 'Faith on the Way' has a structure, has an educational methodology, has deep understandings about spiritual development, has the experience of marking stages in faith with liturgies and – the surprise to ourselves – has the experience, through reflection on our work, of ways to stay within the church and be an agent for renewal within our wider society.

Moving on through life is about crossing thresholds. Sometimes we do not recognize that we have moved from seeing things in one way to seeing them in another until long after the events have taken place. On other occasions we become aware that something has changed. We know that, through a new experience, a conversation, a friendship, a birth or bereavement we now experience life in a different way. We move on because we cannot stand still. The pressures and events of our lives make us face new questions and problems each day we live. Some of these are profound and spring us into new understandings of ourselves. On other occasions we, along with legions of others, choose not to face significant issues in our own lives. We become locked in situations, 'stuck' in relationships or in our work until some trigger comes which offers us the chance to move on.

In the 'Faith on the Way' process we have described some of these moments. We have also talked about rites and ceremonies which might celebrate a decision to see things in a different way. Now we want to suggest that our 'Faith on the Way' discovery leads us on to a further discovery. Both as people come into church life and as we look at the characteristics of a church which has vitality, certain dynamic characteristics are present. People responsible for developing the life of a congregation need to be aware of the various constituent parts and of how various borders might be crossed.

The threshold of welcome

There need to be many doors into the worshipping life of a Christian community. The church with only one door which appears to be open is a church which wants members to join only on its own terms. One open door means that a congregation, or really a small group within it, will have decided what will be on offer to newcomers.

A Christian community which has experimented with many open doors describes its life like this:

> We made a deliberate decision to have different welcome events for newcomers each month. It was exhausting but tremendously rewarding. Our welcome events included barbecues, concerts in church, meeting special speakers, learning to ring handbells for an evening, an Epiphany party and a newcomers' lunch. This is what was right for us. It would not have suited every church. We did not have newcomers for every event and used the occasions to invite friends. The most moving times of all were the newcomers' lunches. Here they could talk to one another about joining this and we just felt a modest sense of pride.

An unassuming sense of welcome means that people who want to take the first steps towards the community of faith can find somewhere for the journey to begin. Just as in 'Faith on the Way', those same newcomers can make their own decision as to whether or not to stay. For those who are in the community already, there is the unconscious discipline of listening to the stories of those who have found one of the community doors.

Welcome always needs the word 'appropriate' placed before it in church circles. Too much welcome or too little can be very off-putting. The welcome which is being described here is much more than that of saying the right thing when giving out the hymn books. It is about a sense of valuing those who are searching. It involves a sense of honesty. Many enquirers who say that they have found friendship in a church mean that they have found something which connects with where they are at this point in their lives. Others say they felt a coolness or a complete lack of welcome. At that time in their lives they were looking for something which they could not find. No community can have all doors open for every enquirer at all times in their lives. Churches with sensitive listening and a willingness to create new options for entry into their community are churches where there is the possibility, at the very least, for new places to be created for new searchers with new questions.

The threshold of deepening faith

The decision to take the claims of Christianity seriously is an enormous one to take. This is not the same as deciding to believe all the tenets of the faith. It is a decision to cross a threshold which will involve living as if at least some of the beliefs of Christianity are true. It will involve self-sacrifice. It will involve a mental journey of exploration. It will certainly involve a change in relationships towards some existing friends. It will be the beginning of a gradual conversion which starts from living *as if* some of those claims are true and, by entering into the experience, discovering that truth is a many-layered thing.

We saw in the very first chapter of this book that people learn in very many different ways. Some of these ways are deliberate: 'Give me a book to read.' 'Where can I hear a lecture on that?' 'Is there a group I can join?' 'Can I read that poem, see that play or hear that piece of music?' We use our senses as well as our intellect to experience and to learn.

We saw also in that first chapter that learning is done as much from entering into an activity as by deliberately wanting to find out or to be told. The village church kneeler project can be mirrored in the centre of city life with a drugs rehabilitation project; in the church which organizes a pilgrimage to the Holy Land; and in the church which raises thousands to repair the roof. Learning takes many forms which have to be recognized and nurtured in the church where a deepening of faith is encouraged.

Translated into the life of a local congregation, liveliness will be seen where there are many different opportunities for faith to be explored and deepened.

> Our church was very snooty about the Alpha Course. It is too simplistic, it preaches and teaches. We thought our newcomers were much too sophisticated for that. We tried a taster and they loved it, meal, discussion and all. Without that basic course in the fundamentals of the faith it would have been much more difficult for many of them to enter into discussion about things we had taken for granted for years.

There is only one fundamental requirement: it is that a Christian community will have as one of its basic assumptions that faith will always be open to question and debate. This openness is not aimed at destroying faith. It has as its objective the creation and refinement of the life of a community of believers who live and explore with integrity. It is a place where, every week, someone new says, 'Now *that* I can believe.'

There are long-established congregations which have yet to cross the threshold of deepening of faith. How often have we heard it said, in a critical way, that many adults only have their Sunday School faith on which to sustain a Christian life. Often it is not the faith of simple values but the faith of emotionalism and a Jesus who never cried and bled and died for anybody.

This threshold crossed will show a congregation where many different activities are going on at the same time. It is possible for newcomers and those who want a refresher to join at the same time. In the small, it may well mean not doing the same thing for Advent and Lent and Mothering Sunday or Harvest Festival every year. It will mean an experiment just now and again which will allow members to enter into the experience of others and, in doing so, find their understanding transformed. Learning is rarely deliberate, nor is the deepening of faith. We cannot very often decide to do it. An unselfconscious decision to break with tradition, to explore something new, to ask a question about something which is assumed to be a rock-solid certainty is to enter a process where faith is deepened.

Some congregations are known for their over-activity. Others are known for their atmosphere of quiet prayerfulness. There are churches which attract for their music, others for their free spirit of worship. One of the great breakthroughs in congregational life where there is openness to the possibility of members being on a journey of faith is that many of these characteristics are permissible within *the same church* – if not always in the same *service*. There is a buzz about a church on the move. Translated into action this buzz will be revealed in the many routes available and encouraged where the seeds of faith which God's Spirit has sown can find a ground and an atmosphere where green shoots are allowed to flourish.

The threshold of decision

There are generations of people within our churches who have never felt the need to talk about their faith. There are many individuals who tell of hoping that something special would happen at their confirmation, but it never did. Expressing faith in words is, for very many Christians, a comparatively new thing. Yet a congregation which cannot demonstrate that it stands for something is, in the all-too-familiar phrase, in danger of either standing for nothing or of falling for anything!

A church which is alive is one where its basic beliefs become evident in some way. This may be in its teaching, in its liturgy, in its social outreach or in some other explicit way. A congregation with a real welcome, through many doors and a multi-layered process of deepening of faith is one where a request for commitment will become evident. To the enquirer or to the member, there will be a time when they say, 'I can go along with this.' Others will come to a stage when they cannot: they will decide to leave. Equally, there should be doors which will open to allow them to do this.

In the end, a congregation with a living spirituality will demand commitment from its members. A denomination should be able to do the same. This has to be the case if a disciple church is to follow a Saviour who demands commitment from those who believe in him. Decisions for commitment should not be the characteristic of only one, 'evangelical' type of church. It has to be a characteristic of all churches and congregations who are alive to the possibility of self-examination and change. With no decision for commitment, there is no 'edge' to the faith and an unacceptable, but more comfortable option, to settle for second-best in everything.

> In our church it would have been much too embarrassing for us to give our testimonies. We have hardly ever spoken in church. When we were ready for confirmation each of us sent a postcard to a real, or imagined, friend, 'Dear . . . , at the end of this course and at this point in my life I now believe that . . . ' Our minister put all these together as our believers' creed just for today. It was a wonderfully honest testimony to what we had shared together and to how much we now trusted each other.

A congregation with 'an edge' is not exclusive and discriminating and certainly not sectarian. It is a community which requires continuous journeying but, every now and again, for markers to be put down.

The threshold of life in the Church

For many years we have given great attention to the way in which enquirers are prepared for full membership of the Church. We have spoken with much enthusiasm about the way in which lay members make a journey alongside newcomers. We have talked about the excitement of using rites and of the way in which a new group who have experienced 'Faith on the Way' can revitalize a parish church. What we have not done with enough rigour is to examine in detail the experience of life in a congregation after the excitement of joining has diminished.

The word given to us by the early Church, *mystagogia*, has a certain mysterious status. It has never been given full and extended examination in our current work. It needs that; it needs to become the final great area of catechumenal learning – how do we understand life within the church?; how do we support each other in that life?; and, most importantly, how does life within the church support and equip Christians for lives of service and witness in the world?

New Christians have spoken with enthusiasm about their time after confirmation or baptism and confirmation. The event itself has been described by an enquirer as 'Just like the time before my wedding.' Equally, the experience of receiving communion has been a most moving time for very many people. They speak with a humbling simplicity about the joy and peace they experienced. Those of us who have spent most of our lives within the Church easily forget the excitement and the drama contained within the Eucharist. We have forgotten, or were never able to remember, the excitement and the drama of baptism.

After all the important rites and the joy of shared experience with new-found friends, there comes the ultimate question – how to respond in a fulfilling way to the call which has come from God to become a Christian? What does God want me to do with my life now? It is a key question and should not at first be answered by an invitation to join one of several committees within the church or to take on a number of other practical tasks. However, the pressure is great. A church which has learned to welcome newcomers has also learned to share out responsibilities. It is unlikely to be a parish where the churchwardens have been in office for twenty years and where there is no rotation of members of the PCC. A true exploration of the question of vocation has to include listening for what God might be doing, and asking us to do, in the world.

The threshold of life in the world

The purpose of the Church is not to provide a haven and a self-perpetuating organization for believers. The Church, at least in its congregational and organizational form, exists to enable the worship of God and to equip Christian believers for lives of service and witness in the world. How this threshold is crossed and re-crossed is an area for rich exploration. We stand in a long and distinguished tradition of Christian engagement with the secular world throughout the last century. The 100 years spans the life and work of the Christian Social Union through to the Industrial Mission Association. The introduction of work placements in units of theological education is now much more common. Groupings and associations of Christian professionals and business people are significant networks of support and witness.

What we hope will be developed as part of the further work of 'Faith on the Way' is the wider establishment of the telling of stories, on an accompanied journey, about worries and concerns of the workplace, hospital or school. Across mainland Europe there have been very good experiences of stories from the world of work coming into

the mutual exchange of the welcome and deepening of faith compo-
nents of 'Faith on the Way'. A great new challenge is to bring within
the life of the local congregation this concern about how to live a life
of faith within the complexities of the modern world. If this can
happen, in the 101 small personal ways which our members know,
then the attempt to broaden 'Faith on the Way' to become a template
for life in all of our church will not have been in vain.

A question for us all

How to live within the church is a question which every Christian
will have asked themselves at one time or another. Some have discovered the question to be a liberating one and have chosen to leave. The
latest trend in England seems to be that attendance patterns are
changing. A way to give breathing space and a way to balance all the
other pressures of life has been to attend church, at least on Sunday,
in a less regular way. Peter Brearley's *The Tide is Running Out* (2000)
demonstrated this change in attendance patterns very clearly indeed.

How to live within the church, and how to run a church with this
kind of life, poses new questions for church leaders, clergy and the
more committed. Many of those who experience the rest of their life
as dynamic and in a constant state of change gradually come to feel a
sense of frustration with the Church as it changes in a very slow way.
The sense of journey so much encouraged by 'Faith on the Way' can
easily become diminished if great energy is put into a church which
takes more than the enthusiasm of newcomers to adapt in any way.
How to stay on in the church and find a fulfilling life within its congregations is a real question for all too many people.

A threshold solution

One of the frequent experiences of conference-goers is the liberation
of finding a group of people with similar concerns about deepening
of faith, about spirituality, about faith at work or about the future of
the Church. Alongside the changing patterns of attendance there
now seems to be a new feature. Active Christian people look beyond
the local church for continuing nurture and support. The growth of
the retreat movement is one example of this. Malcolm has been
working for a number of years with the Third Order of the Society of

St Francis, a lay movement which has trebled in size over the past few years. Those who go to Iona, to Lee Abbey and Scargill, those who visit Taizé and who attend special Taizé services are part of this movement. So, perhaps, are those who belong to the Prayer Book Society and the Latin Mass Society. How to live in the Church and how to find 'survival kits' to be able to stay within the Church is an intriguing question. It is one which has emerged as we have expanded the difficulties and frustrations of the delightful concept of *mystagogia*. It certainly does not mean 'and they lived happily ever after'.

Faith on the way

The story told in this book is our own personal story. It is also the story of many congregations throughout the world. Through God's grace, it is a story of ecumenical co-operation. It is a story about where we are now in a Church which is, as ever, in a process of change and adaptation. In a much more open world, with ease of communication, people will find many sources from which to draw their spirituality. We hope that the local congregation will continue to be the place where community is found and where newcomers are both welcomed and initiated.

We began by saying that the Bible story which inspires our work is that of Jesus walking with the disciples on the Road to Emmaus. It might be appropriate for us to end by saying that the faith story we discover is that which Jesus told about finding the pearl of great price (Matthew 13:45). The merchant was searching for fine pearls; when he found what he was looking for, he went and sold all that he had in order to purchase it. This is the experience of our ministries. Once we discovered that 'Faith on the Way' leads to the priceless pearl of a deeper faith, we knew that this is what we wanted.

Shared stories lead to shared, common understandings of human experience. It is our belief, a part of our faith, that these shared experiences lead to a deepened understanding of the life of the human spirit. Our faith confirms in us the knowledge that a God who goes before us leads us on in an accompanied journey. 'Faith on the Way' is what we have to offer. As ever, it leads us on to new questions and to friends, old and new, who will walk with us along this way.

References and further reading

Ball, Peter, *Journey into Faith* (SPCK, 1984).

Ball, Peter, *Adult Believing: a Guide to the Christian Initiation of Adults* (Mowbray, 1988).

Ball, Peter, *Adult Way to Faith: a Practical Handbook, with Resources to Copy* (Mowbray, 1992).

Ball, Peter, *Journey into Truth: Spiritual Direction in the Anglican Tradition* (Mowbray, 1996).

Brearley, Peter, *The Tide is Running Out* (Christian Research, 2000).

Grundy, Malcolm, *Evangelization Through the Adult Catechumenate* (Grove Books, 1991).

Grundy, Malcolm, *Understanding Congregations* (Mowbray, 1998).

On the Way: Towards an Integrated Approach to Christian Initiation (Church House Publishing, 1995).

ELEVEN

RESOURCES

REMEMBER ALWAYS that the strongest and most fruitful resource that any parish or institution has is the actual people who travel together on the way. The whole process relies on their openness to the activity of God's Holy Spirit in them. God works through men and women as they reflect on their experience of life and on the living Christian inheritance. God is there in their intention to find his presence and will. That conviction lies at the heart of all we have written in this book.

Not all leaders of groups or people accompanying enquirers will feel able at the start to launch out into this journey without help. In the worksheets we have given some ideas for local preparation in this ministry. There are also a number of different resources which are readily available.

Networks

In the United Kingdom, the Catechumenate Network provides an opportunity for Anglicans and others to meet and learn from one another at regular training days and conferences. It is one of the organizations which jointly publish *Ministry* several times a year. The correspondent is Mr Andrew Harter, Tithings New Barn, Swalclifffe, Banbury, OX15 5DR.

The Roman Catholic Church in England and Wales has its RCIA Network. The contact is Mrs Veronica Murphy, 5 Gerald Road, Pendleton, Salford, M6 6DL.

Every two years the European Conference on the Adult Catechumenate meets to exchange information and develop the work of the catechumenate. Its membership consists of people from the Catholic churches of most Western European countries together with Anglicans and Swedish Lutherans. The secretariat is provided by the French Service National du Catéchuménat, 4 avenue Vavin, 75006 Paris.

The North American Forum on the Catechumenate offers comprehensive training institutes for various aspects of the catechumenate and publishes a regular journal. The address is The North American Forum on the Catechumenate, 3033 Fourth Street NE, Washington DC 20017-1102, USA. The Office of Evangelism Ministries of the Episcopal Church is based at the Episcopal Church Center, 815 Second Avenue, New York, NY 10017. The North American Association for the Catechumenate caters for Episcopalians, Lutherans and others in the USA and Canada. The contact address is 128 Summit Glen Road, Pataskaia, Ohio 46082.

In Australia several dioceses have their own networks. The General Board of Religious Education provides national links. The address is GBRE, PO Box 535, Boronia, VIC 3155.

The address for contacting the Swedish Catechumenate Network is: Sommarstate, S-341 91 LJUNGBY.

Books on the process

The Rite of Christian Initiation of Adults: A Study Book (St Thomas More Centre, London, 1988) gives the official Roman Catholic text and provides commentaries on its use.

The Book of Occasional Services: Second Edition (The Church Hymnal Corporation, New York, 1988) contains official Anglican services and directions for the catechumenate, produced by the Episcopal Church's Standing Liturgical Commission. Under the title *Welcome to Christ* the Lutheran Churches of North America have produced three short books, *A Lutheran Introduction to the Catechumenate, Lutheran Rites for the Catechumenate* and *A Lutheran Catechetical Guide* (Augsburg Fortress, Minneapolis, 1997).

John W. B. Hill, *Making Disciples: Serving Those who are Entering the Christian Life* (The Hoskin Group, Toronto, 1991) offers an 'Order for Catechesis', outlining a pastoral ministry to use with people entering the Christian faith and liturgies to celebrate their conversion journey.

Thomas H. Morris, *The RCIA. Transforming the Church. A Resource for Pastoral Implementation* (Paulist Press, New York, 1989) is by a previous Director of the North American Forum. It is written from a base of experience in the catechumenate and of accompanying people into Christian faith and committed ministry in the world.

Malcolm Grundy's *Evangelization Through the Adult Catechumenate* (Grove Books, Nottingham, 1991) is a short handbook on the

Adult Way to Faith, recommended as an introduction for lay people in the parish.

James B. Dunning, *New Wine, New Wineskins* (Sadlier, New York, 1981) is one of the early American books giving a clear and attractive introduction to the process. His *Echoing God's Word* (National Forum on the Catechumenate, 1993) is a powerful training manual for people involved in the process.

The Hallelujah Highway: A History of the Catechumenate by Paul Turner helps people enter the story, from St Peter to the present day. He has also written *The Catechumenate Answer Book: Modern Liturgy Answers the 101 Most Asked Questions*. This book follows the sequence of events along the enquirer's journey.

Mary Birmingham offers an excellent resource for leaders in three volumes of her *Word and Worship Workbook: For Ministry in Initiation, Preaching, Religious Education and Formation* (Paulist Press, 1998). She works from the Lectionary's three years and the celebration of liturgy and provides material which encourages groups to do their own work on the readings and the events of worship.

In Australia the General Board of Religious Education has produced *Using the Catechumenal Process in Australia; A Guide for the Initiation and Formation of Adults in the Anglican Church* (GBRE, 1999). It is a clear and comprehensive manual for introducing and supporting the work and also contains leaflets with liturgies for the stages of the journey.

Anyone who is interested in getting down to some real study will find Maxwell E. Johnson's *The Rites of Christian Initiation; Their Evolution and Interpretation* an extremely useful source book. A Pueblo book published in 1999 by The Liturgical Press, it describes the development of the rites from New Testament times to the present day and gives a full treatment of the Catechumenate, both in the early centuries and in its contemporary use in Roman Catholic, Anglican and Lutheran churches.

Background

William Abraham, *The Logic of Evangelism* (Hodder & Stoughton, London, 1989) offers creative and critical insights into the theory and practice of evangelism today, giving full weight to the process of conversion and personal journey.

How Faith Grows: Faith Development and Christian Education (National Society/Church House Publishing, London, 1991) relates the insights of such writers as James W. Fowler to the work of churches and schools. (James Fowler is the author of *Stages of Faith* and *Becoming Adult, Becoming Christian*.)

John Finney's *Finding Faith Today* (British and Foreign Bible Society, 1992) provides important survey evidence of the way people come to faith.

The Tide is Running Out by Peter Brearley (Christian Research, 2000) gives the latest information about church attendance in England, with analysis and ideas about ways forward.

Adult Christian education

In *Learning for Life: A Handbook of Adult Religious Education* (Mowbray, 1994) Yvonne Craig provides exactly what her subtitle promises, *A Handbook of Adult Religious Education*. It is an essential tool for a parish embarking on this process.

Patrick Purnell (ed.), *To be a People of Hope* (Collins, 1987) is not only a book about adult education, but an aid in enabling the process to happen.

Emmaus: The Way of Faith (National Society/Church House Publishing, 1996) provides a training course in several volumes, with strong links to the catechumenal process.

Malcolm Grundy, *Understanding Congregations* (Mowbray Parish Handbooks, Mowbray, 1998), offers a searching insight into the life of local church communities.

In *Journey into Truth: Spiritual Direction in the Anglican Tradition* (Mowbray, 1996) and *Anglican Spiritual Direction* (Cowley Publications, Boston, 1998), Peter Ball offers a survey of Anglican spiritual direction over the centuries. The books are designed to be an accessible resource for people who accompany others on their journey.

Group Spiritual Direction: Community for Discernment (Paulist Press, 1995) by Rose Marie Dougherty, SSND, provides practical guidance for offering and participating in spiritual direction in the setting of a small group.

In *Ministry in Three Dimensions*, Steven Croft (Darton, Longman & Todd, 1999) looks at ministry and development in the local church from an evangelical standpoint.

Robin Greenwood's *Transforming Priesthood and Practising Community* (SPCK, 1994, 1996) reviews the theology of ministry and life in the local church.

APPENDIX:
ADULT CATECHUMENATE AND RCIA
– A COMMON EXPERIENCE

A briefing paper written for the International meeting of Anglican and Roman Catholic Bishops, held in Missisauga, near Toronto in May 2000, on the shared experiences of our Churches

Background

Ever since the mid-1980s there have been close personal links between those developing the Rite of Christian Initiation of Adults in the Roman Catholic Church and a group of enthusiasts within the Church of England working in what has become the Adult Catechumenate Network.

We have shared in one another's national conferences. We have travelled together and shared experiences at the European Meetings of those developing the Catechumenate. Strong bonds of friendship have been established. These have been reinforced as conversations developed about problems and questions as well as in our discussions about the educational methods we are using.

The RCIA has a more formal structure and has received resources from most dioceses in England and Wales. The support and teaching from Parish Catechists, linked directly into Initiation Rites, some conducted in parishes, and the Rite of Election with the Bishop in his cathedral give the appearance of a confident overarching structure. The Adult Catechumenate has gradually won a place for itself in Anglican practice. This reached a peak with the publication of a report commissioned by the House of Bishops called *On the Way*. Experiences such as these are paralleled, with variations, in the Episcopal Church of the USA, the Church in South Africa and the Church in Australia. All of our courses are scripturally based and great emphasis has been placed on 'listening to the Bible'. Many programmes follow readings in the weekly lectionary.

We also found that, even though the RCIA had an 'official' status, we each shared issues and concerns about how to relate our experience of the work on the ground to the more formalized structures of our Churches. In a different way, we have found ourselves brought closer together through shared concerns about other programmes and courses which have developed in recent years and have become very popular means of bringing adult enquirers into a deeper faith.

For the last two years we have put our meetings on an 'official' basis. This has been particularly beneficial as we begin to work together to plan the next European Conference in England in the year 2001.

A common process of learning

If we are to be strictly honest, there was a time in the mid-1990s when we both began to feel overtaken by other teaching methods in our Churches. It was felt that many Catholic parishes were only paying 'lip service' to the RCIA in its mainstream recommended method of use. Anglican parishes were turning to the more professionally packaged and promoted Alpha and Emmaus courses.

Our early joint meetings were characterized by a sharing of these experiences. There was almost a feeling that what we had promoted had appealed to a previous generation of parish teachers and diocesan trainers who had placed more focus on structured but experiential faith sharing.

This mood was short-lived. We began to take our own medicine and use the methods of reflecting on experience which we had long commended to others. What has emerged is an ability to distance ourselves from any particular course. We have asked what have to be the essential ingredients of any course or programme which is designed to welcome newcomers to the faith and which provides a mixture of knowledge and experience. Our shared journey of exploration has enabled us to express our understandings in a particular language.

Convergence

We used the language of ecumenical dialogue to state our different experiences and then to evaluate where we see similarities and moments of learning. We looked at the documents and training materials which we have developed and, with very little need for adaptation, we found that we could recognize the same basic concepts about the need to listen to enquirers, to begin with them, and that shared journey and story were important. We saw the same need to mark stages of faith by ceremonies or rites. We found that it was essential to use lay members of congregations to accompany enquirers. We discovered the supportive role of parish priests to be essential but difficult for them to grasp. We shared a belief in the importance of the need for the wider Church, through the Bishop, to take a central part in the welcoming of the newly-committed.

Pockets of good practice

We discovered that we were coming to our common discoveries in a particularly revealing way. This was not the enthusiastic Anglicans, with hardly any materials, talking and listening to Roman Catholics from a Church with a national strategy and workers in every diocese. We found that the pearls of great price were hidden in the parishes which had taken the Catechumenal process seriously. By allowing an exchange of experience and good practice from parishes and advisers we discovered our common language and common concepts.

Similarities in our dioceses and parishes

It is no secret that very many clergy and even more lay parish teachers long for the ideal course or package which they can take from a book-shelf and use in the Parish Room. No such courses exist. We discovered that we had been saying this to our people for years.

Clergy are tremendously reluctant to let lay people in their parishes teach enquirers. Either they are jealous that the orthodoxy of the faith will be distorted – or they are jealous that they cannot engage in 'real' teaching with 'real' adults themselves. An understandable insecurity was what we each discovered in our clergy. We also discovered how we were able to encourage and support, thorough the introduction of shared experience, a new confidence between tentative parishes and ones where eyes lit up with the joy of the experience.

We have also found, even in the most supportive parishes, that the able and willing lay people we have are already overburdened with 'churchy' tasks and that it is hard to put more on them. We also discovered how hard it is to get newcomers trusted with work when established patterns and roles already exist in a parish.

Key stages

Taking established educational concepts from the world of school education we have reflected on our processes and decided that it is possible to offer a critique with key stages and key elements in any Faith Development Programme. We now want to offer these as the fruits of what twenty years of joint Adult Catechumenate and RCIA work can offer to the wider Church.

Any course, however structured or however free-ranging, will have as its first key stage a time and process of *welcome*. Here enquirers will discover that they are being listened to and that their questions are heard. Here initial trust is established

There will then be a marked threshold crossing into a time when faith is *deepened* by teaching and by open discussion.

At a particular point, more often determined by the enquirers than the teachers, there will come a time for *commitment* with a public profession of faith and a liturgy of initiation from the mother Church.

Everyone, especially the learners, by this stage have only just begun to learn how to learn and how much more they need and want to learn. So the final shared concept is that the catechumenal process is ultimately about discovering the excitement of *lifelong learning*.

Any parish which attempts to rush this process by starting without a welcome or by leapfrogging any stage will fail. The result will, at best, be partly formed new Christians, certainly church members who remain unmoved in their certainties with unacknowledged and unasked questions of their own, and, at worst, unaffirmed and frustrated clergy 'stuck' in patterns of learning they have brought with them from school, college, university or seminary.

Achievements

In our twenty years of work together promoting the methods of the Catechumenate we are now able to reflect on considerable achievement from those who have experienced this method of becoming adult Christians. Because the process involves continuous dialogue between enquirers and lay Christians there has developed a strong sense that church members can relate to the culture around them. They have learned to do this in a language which can be understood by those outside. Because the aim of the work it to draw enquirers into the church community, many have discovered their truer identity in forging these relationships. The Adult Catechumenate/ RCIA digs deeper and does not produce 'pew fodder'. Within many parishes there have emerged collaborative teams who are creating a new model for the local church.

Further work

Our joint experience has led us to the conclusion that there is one area where, with hindsight, we would have given more emphasis. In common with most English congregations there is a new area of common concern. With the less than weekly attendance at church by many committed people, new forms of support need to be developed. We call the time after baptism, confirmation or full commitment *Mystagogia*, a term borrowed from the early Church. We now realize that a much more sophisticated system of support and further dialogue is needed to enable the committed to continue to deepen their lay discipleship. The less frequent attendance, with its consequent less frequent reception of the sacrament, is changing or has already changed the structure of the local congregation and the relationship of the priest to the people. We will be attempting to explore this issue in our continuing dialogue. We hope that from this there will emerge some new practice which can be offered more widely to the churches.

This Appendix has been written by the Ven. Malcolm Grundy, in consultation with other members of the Joint Working Group (*Anglicans:* Canon Peter Ball, The Revd Sandy Railton, The Revd Nicholas Henshall. *Roman Catholics:* The Revd Gerry Murphy, The Revd Paul Billington, Sister Mary Brennan, Mrs Veronica Murphy, Mr Derek Titchen).